The Belief of Isma'il

Second Edition

Adan Ibn Isma'il

First Edition Published 2003
Reprinted with minor corrections 2004
Reprinted with minor corrections 2006
Reprinted 2007
Reprinted with minor corrections 2009
Second Edition Published 2022

Printed in the United States of America

I would like to express my extreme gratitude to Dawud Muhammad and his daughter Khadijah Laila and to Tamid Chaidir and Ali Rahman for all of their help in reviewing and editing this book. I thank all my friends who have encouraged and prayed for me as I wrote this book. I also thank Rajaah Khalid for the additional suggestions and corrections used in the book. May Allah (swt) bless all of us!

For the Second Edition, special mention and thanks are due to Ali Rahman, Jaffar Abdul-Hayy, and Basheer Abdul-Rahman for all of their work in developing this revised and expanded edition. Thanks also to the other members of the team who reviewed and offered additional suggestions and encouragement in this effort.

Bismillahir rahmanir rahim

Assalamu'alaikum wa rahmatullahi wa barakatuh

أَهْدِنَا ٱلصِّرَٰطَ ٱلْمُسْتَقِيمَ

Show us The Straight way

Will they not ponder the Qur'an, or are there locks upon their hearts?

(Muhammad 47:24[1])

May Allah (swt) enlighten your heart.

Contents

❖ ෨෬෨෬෨෬෨෬෨෬෨෬ ❖

Chapter 1: Problems

My name is Isma'il. I'm a Muslim from a large Muslim family in a Muslim country. I've been working as a schoolteacher for several years. I have a very close friend named Abdullah. Abdullah and I live in the same village. We've been friends since we were young. We grew up together, played together, went to school together, and as adults we even took holidays together. We've been such good friends, so naturally we can talk to each other about whatever's happening in our lives or anything else we want. I like talking about spiritual things. Here's an example of some typical conversations I might have with my Muslim friend Abdullah.

Isma'il: Assalamu'alaikum, Abdullah!

Abdullah: Wa'alaikum salam wa-rahmatullah wa-barakatuh! How are you, Isma'il?

Isma'il: Alhamdulillah, I'm fine. How about you?

Abdullah: I'm okay, but I have a lot of problems. It seems like I always have problems, and I don't know how to solve them.

Isma'il: I'm sorry to hear that, Abdullah. I hope that things get better for you. Problems are a part of life, but you don't always have to carry them alone. Why don't you tell me about your problems? Who knows, I might be able to help you.

Abdullah: Thanks! You know what? When I look at you, you always look happy. It seems that you don't have as many problems in your life as I do. Why is that?

Isma'il: Of course I have problems, but I always ask Allah (swt) to help me.

Abdullah: Hmm,… Every time we have a conversation, you always involve Allah (swt). You're so religious, Isma'il.

Isma'il: No, Abdullah, I'm not just religious, but I also believe in putting my trust in Allah (swt).

Abdullah: What do you mean? What's the difference?

Isma'il: I discovered more about Allah (swt) through studying the Qur'an. The Qur'an taught me that I should **learn** about **how to live** my **life from the lives of the prophets** that Allah (swt) sent.

Abdullah: You mean from the prophet Muhammad (pbuh), right?

Isma'il: Of course, from the prophet Muhammad (pbuh), but we have to **learn from the other prophets** too. Remember, the Qur'an teaches us that we have to **believe in all the prophets of Allah** (swt). As it says in the Qur'an,

Say, "We believe in Allah and what was revealed to us and what was revealed to Ibrahim, Ismail, Ishaq, Yaqub, and the tribes, what was given to Musa and Isa, and what was given to the prophets from their Lord. We do not distinguish between any of them, and we are submitted to him." (Al-Baqarah 2:136)

Abdullah: I was also taught that we have to believe in Allah (swt), angels, the Holy Books, the messengers, and the Day of Judgment.

Isma'il: That's right, it says that in the Qur'an. In one ayah (verse), it says,

"Righteousness is not a matter of turning your faces eastward or westward. Rather, **righteousness is believing** in Allah and the Last Day and the angels and the Book and the prophets; ..." (Al-Baqarah 2:177)

In another ayah, it says,

"Believers, believe in Allah, his messenger, the book he revealed to his messenger, and the book he revealed beforehand. Whoever disbelieves in Allah, his angels, his books, his messengers and the last day has gone far astray." (Al-Nisa 4:136)

Abdullah: I truly appreciate how you know the Qur'an so well.

Isma'il: Alhamdulillah. As Muslims, we should do more than just reciting the Qur'an. We need to study the Qur'an too. Sometimes I didn't understand the classical Arabic used in the Qur'an, but still I didn't give up on studying the Qur'an. Thankfully I was able to find some books to help me better understand the Arabic of the Qur'an. As I continued to study, I found many blessings in the Qur'an, and because of that **I don't have to worry about anything**.

Abdullah: Yes, but...

Isma'il: But what, Abdullah?

Abdullah: There's something that I worry about. I'm afraid of what will happen to me when I die.

Isma'il: You mean like on the Day of Judgment?

Abdullah: Yes.

Isma'il: Why are you afraid?

Abdullah: Well, Isma'il, you've known me for a long time. You know how I always try to obey all the rules: I pray five times a day, I observe Ramadan and do fasting, and zakat – giving money to the poor. So, people think of me as a pretty good person.

Isma'il: All of those things are good if you believe and have faith in Allah (swt). So, what's the problem?

Abdullah: The problem is, even though I obey all the rules, there's still something missing.

Isma'il: What is it, Abdullah?

Abdullah: I don't have peace in my heart. When I die, I'm not sure if I'll end up in paradise or in hell, so I'm afraid of dying.

Isma'il: Oh, I see. Perhaps it's because you haven't found **the Straight Way** yet. **Do you know** what **the Straight Way** is?

Abdullah: The Straight Way? I know the phrase and recite it a lot. What do you mean by it?

Isma'il: You said that you were afraid of dying because you don't know what will happen to you on the Day of Judgment and if you'll enter paradise after you die. Can I share something with you?

Abdullah: Ok.

Isma'il: If we **know the Straight Way, we don't have to worry about our future**.

Abdullah: How's that?

Isma'il: We pray five times a day, and we recite the Al-Fatihah in numerous rakats (cycles of prayer), right?

Abdullah: Yes, that's correct.

Isma'il: In Al-Fatihah, 1:6, it says, "Show us the Straight Way."[2] So how many times a day do we ask Allah (swt) to show us the Straight Way?

Abdullah: Twice in the morning (Fajr), four times in the middle of the day (Dhuhr), four times in the afternoon ('Asr), three times in the evening (Maghrib), and four times at night ('Isha). So that's seventeen times a day.

Isma'il: So, seventeen times a day, we ask Allah (swt) to show us the Straight Way. Do you know what the Straight Way is?

Abdullah: I'm not sure.

Isma'il: It's in the Qur'an. It says,

> "**He [*Isa*] is knowledge of the hour** [*of judgment*], so do not doubt it, and follow me. **This is a straight path**. ... When **Isa** brought miracles, he **said**, 'I have come to you with wisdom, and to clarify to you your differences, so **fear Allah and obey me**. Allah is my Lord and your Lord, so worship him. **This is a straight path**.'" (Al-Zukhruf 43:61, 63-64)

Abdullah: Oh, I didn't remember that ayah (verse).

Isma'il: In that case, I'm glad that I recited the ayat (verses) about the Straight Way. Not only does **the Straight Way** refer to worshipping and revering Allah (swt), but it also means that we have to **obey and follow Isa al-Masih** (as). Allah promised that if we follow Isa (as), we will be exalted in this world and the next. As it says in the Qur'an,

> Allah said, "Isa, **I will** make you die and raise you up to me, and purify you from the disbelievers, and **make your followers higher than the disbelievers** until the day of resurrection. ..." (Aal Imran 3:55)

All of this is part of the Straight Way.

Abdullah: What do you mean, obey and follow Isa al-Masih (as)??? Isn't Isa al-Masih (as) only for Christians?

Isma'il: Of course not, Abdullah! Isa al-Masih (as) is for everyone, including **for Muslims** too. **Isa** (as) **is a Muslim**!

Abdullah: No way! Are you serious?

Isma'il: I'm not kidding, Abdullah. Do you know **the meaning of** the word **Muslim**? And can you tell me the definition of **Islam**?

Abdullah: Islam is a religion, and a Muslim is someone who practices that religion, right?

Isma'il: It's more than just that. Islam and Muslim both mean to **submit or surrender to Allah** (swt). Based on the Qur'an, I believe that **Isa al-Masih** (as) is someone who has **submitted and surrendered to Allah** (swt). For example, Isa (as) is a servant of Allah (swt).

> "He said, "I am Allah's servant. ..." (Mariam 19:30)

Abdullah: Okay, but just because someone is a servant doesn't mean they want to be or that they always do what their master wants them to.

Isma'il: That's correct. But in the Qur'an, it also says,

> "The Messiah will not disdain to be a servant of Allah, nor will the angels who have been brought near. ..." (Al-Nisa 4:172)

A true servant is someone with a servant's heart who is truly submitted to his master. Look at the attitude of Isa (as) in contrast with those who don't submit to Allah (swt). Isa's (as) attitude is one of submission. He isn't too proud to be Allah's (swt) servant. He doesn't consider it beneath his dignity. I also believe that **Isa al-Masih** (as) must be someone who has **submitted and surrendered to Allah** (swt), especially since **his followers have also submitted to Allah** (swt). So that's another reason I think **Isa** (as) **was a Muslim**. There's an ayah in the Qur'an that says,

"When Isa sensed their disbelief, he said, 'Who are my helpers toward Allah?' The disciples [*hawariyun*] said, 'We are Allah's helpers. We have believed in Allah, so **testify that we have submitted**.'" (Aal Imran 3:52)

Abdullah: So, Muslims should follow Isa al-Masih (as) too?

Isma'il: Yes, of course, Abdullah. Do you know who **the first Muslim** was **to believe in Isa al-Masih** (as) **after the Qur'an was revealed**?

Abdullah: You?

Isma'il: Me? No, Abdullah. The first Muslim to believe in Isa al-Masih (as) after the Qur'an was revealed was **the prophet Muhammad** (pbuh)! He recited many ayat for us about Isa. In fact, **Isa al-Masih** (as) **is referred to in more than 90 ayat in the Qur'an**.

Abdullah: So why did Allah (swt) have the prophet Muhammad (pbuh) tell us so much about Isa al-Masih (as)?

Isma'il: Because, the prophet **Muhammad** (pbuh) came as **a warner**. He warned us about the terrible torments in Hell that await those who have been disobedient and those who have gone astray. **He brought us the message about Allah's** (swt) **mercy for us**.

Abdullah: Hmm,... I suppose Allah (swt) might love some people, but I'm not sure if I'm good enough for Allah (swt) to love me. I need to be pure for Allah (swt) to love me. I'm trying to be good, but sometimes I fail.

Isma'il: But Abdullah, we can never make ourselves pure. **Only Allah** (swt) **can make us pure**. I learned that from the Qur'an. It says,

"Believers, do not follow Satan's footsteps. Satan commands those who follow his footsteps to do promiscuous, immoral things. If **Allah's grace and mercy** had not been on you, none of you would ever be pure, but **Allah purifies** those He wills. Allah hears all and knows all." (An-Nur 24:21)

Since that's the case, we should pray and **ask Allah** (swt) **to show** us **His favor and mercy, and** to **purify us**.

Abdullah: Well, to be perfectly honest, I have to admit that I've made a few mistakes, and I've been disobedient sometimes, but only a little bit. On the other hand, I've done a lot of good deeds too. So when I die, if I can show Allah (swt) that **I've done many good deeds**

and only a few mistakes, then hopefully Allah (swt) will be gracious and merciful to me and let me into paradise.

Isma'il: Abdullah, my friend, Allah (swt) is Holy and Pure. As the Qur'an says,

> **"He is Allah**. He is the only god, King, **Holy**, Peace, Faithful, Sovereign, Mighty, Almighty, and Proud. May Allah be glorified above the gods they worship." (Al-Hashr 59:23)

> "Everything in the heavens and on the earth worships **Allah, the holy king**, mighty and wise." (Al-Jumuah 62:1)

> Do you know what the word "holy" means?

Abdullah: Not exactly.

Isma'il: Holy means to be completely pure and clean. It means to be free from everything that is unbefitting to Allah (swt). Allah (swt) looks at our hearts and at our deeds.

Abdullah: Ok. But even though Allah (swt) is Holy, won't He accept me?

Isma'il: Yes, but only **if you are completely pure**! Like it said in the ayah I quoted before,

> "... If **Allah's grace and mercy** had not been on you, none of you would ever be pure, but **Allah purifies** those He wills. Allah hears all and knows all." (An-Nur 24:21)

> Abdullah, as I told you before, Allah (swt) is Holy and Pure, so we can only be accepted if we are totally pure. But do you truly believe anyone can be that pure?

Abdullah: Maybe it's possible.

Isma'il: Are you sure? Let me give you an example, so you can understand my point. When you visit my house, I always offer you a glass of fresh, clean water. You know the water is very clean since you watched me boil it. So, you'd drink it without doubting its purity, right?

Abdullah: Of course.

Isma'il: But what if you knew that there was a very, very, tiny speck of mouse droppings in your glass? You'd still drink it, wouldn't you? After all, it's not much, just a tiny speck of droppings from the mouse.

Abdullah: No way! I wouldn't drink it!

Isma'il: Why not?

Abdullah: There are mouse droppings in it! The water is dirty!

Isma'il: So, you'd refuse the water because it has a minute speck of mouse droppings, but you expect pure and holy Allah (swt) to accept your misdeeds? That's why no matter how many good things we've done, **we can't come to Allah** (swt) **with anything unbefitting to Him**. Even the smallest mistakes **Allah** (swt) **will judge**.

Abdullah: Do you really believe Allah (swt) is that strict?

Isma'il: Yes. The Qur'an tells us about the consequences of our misdeeds. It says,

"... Those [*unbelievers*] who lived before them behaved in the same way. God [*Allah*] did not wrong them. They wronged themselves. **They were struck by the consequences of the evil they had done**, and they were overtaken by the very thing they used to ridicule." (Al-Nahl 16:33-34[1])

According to another ayah,

"Whoever comes to his Lord as an evildoer is destined for Hell where he will neither die nor live." (Taha 20:74[1])

Abdullah: That's terrible!

Isma'il: So, it's only by **the Compassion and Mercy of Allah** (swt) that we can be clean.

Abdullah: I see.

Isma'il: Do you know who **the predestined Mercy of Allah** (swt) is?

Abdullah: I'm not sure.

Isma'il: We're told that before Isa was born, Allah (swt) sent His spirit to Maryam (ra).

"He said, "This is your Lord's saying: 'It is easy for me, so we will make him [*Isa*] **a sign for people, and a mercy from us. This was a predestined matter**.'" (Mariam 19:21)

Abdullah: I heard someone say that Isa al-Masih (as) only came for the Jews, right?

Isma'il: Well Abdullah, remember what it says in the ayah. Notice the words "**a sign for people**". It doesn't say a sign to the Jews, right? It **means a sign for everybody, all people**.

Abdullah: Anyway, Isma'il, there's something else I wanted to ask you. It seems that you don't have as many problems in your life as I do. But if I ever see you having problems, you always do a good job solving them.

Isma'il: No, Abdullah. I **can't solve my problems by my own power**, but Allah (swt) helps me. **Allah** (swt) has **promised victory to people who believe and follow Isa al-Masih** (as), **and** He has promised **to exalt them**. In the Qur'an it says,

"... **We** [*Allah*] **aided the believers** [*in Isa*] **against their enemy, and they were victorious**." (Al-Saff 61:14)

"Allah said, '**Isa, I will** ... **make your followers higher than the disbelievers** until the day of resurrection. ...'" (Aal Imran 3:55)

Well, Abdullah, based on the Qur'an, I believe the enemy is Satan and his followers. They always attack us with all sorts of problems in our daily life. As the Qur'an says,

"Satan is your enemy, so treat him as an enemy. His call on his followers (will only lead them) to be among those of the Blazing Fire." (Fatir 35:6[1])

But, alhamdulillah, I can overcome all the problems in this life because Isa helps me.

Abdullah: I feel perplexed by all this talk about believing, obeying, and following Isa al-Masih (as). It seems strange to me for a good Muslim like you to talk so much about Isa al-Masih (as).

Isma'il: I don't think it's strange because **there are many stories about the life of Isa al-Masih** (as) **in the Qur'an**. Besides that, we as Muslims have to **read the entire Qur'an**. So, of course we have to read all of the ayat about Isa al-Masih (as). It would be **wrong** for a Muslim **to skip the ayat about Isa al-Masih** (as). Well, Abdullah, I know you read the Qur'an, right?

Abdullah: Yes, of course I read it and recite it, but it's in classical Arabic, so I don't always understand it very well. I wish the Qur'an was in modern Arabic so I could understand it better.

Isma'il: Why not get some help? There are dictionaries of classic Arabic to explain the words in modern Arabic, and you can go to almost any bookstore and find a Qur'an with tafsir (commentary) or even books of tafsir on the Qur'an.

Abdullah: How is it that you know so much about Isa al-Masih (as)?

Isma'il: I know about Isa al-Masih (as) because **there are a lot of ayat about Isa al-Masih** (as) **in the Qur'an**.

Abdullah: But since Muhammad (pbuh) has come, why do we need to learn about Isa al-Masih (as)?

Isma'il: You know there are many Muslims who **ignore** reading about Isa al-Masih (as). They think that since Muhammad (pbuh) was the last prophet, there's no longer a reason to be interested in learning about the life of Isa al-Masih (as) or any of the other prophets. But I believe that **based on how much Isa** (as) **is referred to in the Qur'an, we should be very interested in the life of Isa al-Masih** (as).

Abdullah: So why does the Qur'an tell us so many things about Isa al-Masih (as)?

Isma'il: It's because **Isa al-Masih** (as) **is very different from all the other prophets**.

Abdullah: Different? What makes you think Isa al-Masih (as) is so special? I mean, you must since you keep telling me that we have to learn about the life of Isa al-Masih (as) and that we have to obey and follow him. What makes him different?

Isma'il: How do I know Isa al-Masih (as) is so special? Well, Abdullah, the Qur'an tells us that Allah (swt) sent angels to announce to Maryam (ra) that **Isa al-Masih** (as) would be **highly exalted in this world and the Hereafter**. The Qur'an says,

"When the angels said, 'Mariam, Allah gives you good news of a word from him, whose name will be the Messiah, **Isa** son of Mariam, **highly exalted in this world and the hereafter, and brought near [to Allah]**.'" (Aal Imran 3:45)

Abdullah: I think there's an ayah that says we shouldn't make a distinction between Allah's (swt) messengers. But it seems to me that you're making a distinction between Isa al-Masih (as) and the other prophets by exalting Isa (as).

Isma'il: Perhaps the ayah you're referring to is Al-Baqarah 2:136, which says,

Say, "We believe in Allah and what was revealed to us and what was revealed to Ibrahim, Ismail, Ishaq, Yaqub, and the tribes, what was given to Musa and Isa, and what was given to the prophets from their Lord. We do not distinguish between any of them, and we are submitted to him." (Al-Baqarah 2:136)

This ayah warns us not to make a **distinction**. But I'm not the one who showed a preference by exalting Isa (as). It was **Allah** (swt) Himself who **made the distinction**. According to the Qur'an, Allah (swt) said,

"We preferred some of those messengers, over others. Allah spoke to some, and he raised some in degree: We gave Isa son of Mariam miracles, and aided him with the Holy Spirit. …" (Al-Baqarah 2:253)

So, we can see that it was **Allah** (swt) himself who **preferred some messengers over others**. For example, we know that **Allah** (swt) **spoke to Isa** (as) **directly several times**, according to the Surahs Aal Imran 3:55 and Al-Maidah 5:116. The ayah in Al Imran says,

Allah said, "**Isa, I will** make you die and **raise you up to me**, and purify you from the disbelievers, ..." (Aal Imran 3:55)

Notice Allah (swt) said that He was raising Isa (as) to Himself. Prior to that, in Aal Imran 3:45, Allah's (swt) angels also said that **Isa** (as) would be **highly exalted in this world and the next** and that he would be **near stationed to Allah** (swt). In addition to all of that, **Allah** (swt) **showed His favor to Isa** (as) **by giving him miracles and aiding him with the Holy Spirit**. So it was **Allah** (swt) who **exalted Isa al-Masih** (as).

Abdullah: Oh, I never connected the ayat (verses) in that way before. So Isma'il, can you tell me, what's **the meaning of al-Masih**?

Isma'il: It means "**the anointed one**." Did you know that a long time ago, when there were kings over the Children of Israel, they used to pour oil on the person's head to make him the king? Prophets were also anointed.[5] One of the reasons Isa al-Masih (as) is so special is because **Allah** (swt) **gave Isa** (as) **the title, al-Masih**. This ayah means that **Allah** (swt) **has chosen Isa al-Masih (as) and anointed him**, not just with oil but **with His Spirit**!

Abdullah: Mashallah (amazing). Suppose someone believed in Isa al-Masih (as). Wouldn't he be called a Christian?

Isma'il: Abdullah, you've known me almost my whole life, and you've always known me as an observant Muslim. I remember when we were young; we went together to the mosque. We've fasted together for Ramadan. You've visited my family for Eid al-Fitri, and I've visited your family too. Just because I know and believe in Isa al-Masih (as), nobody calls me a Christian, right? **I'm a Muslim**, and you know that. Besides that, **Isa al-Masih** (as) **never asked people to become Christians. Isa al-Masih** (as) only **asks us to obey and follow him**. As it says in the Qur'an,

> "When **Isa** brought miracles, he **said**, 'I have come to you with wisdom, and to clarify to you your differences, **so fear Allah and obey me**.'" (Al-Zukhruf 43:63)

The Qur'an also tells us that,

> "**Allah said**, '**Isa, I will** make you die and raise you up to me, and purify you from the disbelievers, and **make your followers higher than the disbelievers** until the day of resurrection. Then you will return to me and I will judge between you in matters about which you differ'" (Aal Imran 3:55)

Abdullah: So then, why are there people called Christians today?

Isma'il: I tell you, Abdullah, **Isa** (as) **and his disciples didn't call themselves Christians**. But their opponents started calling them Christians in another country years later after Allah (swt) raised Isa (as) to heaven in Aal Imran 3:55.

Abdullah: How do you know?

Isma'il: You can look it up for yourself online.

Abdullah: Isma'il, you know a lot about Isa al-Masih (as), and you always like to talk about Allah (swt), even to our neighbors who are Christians. I know some Muslims don't want to talk with Christians. I was wondering how you could be so open and friendly with so many different kinds of people, especially with Christians, since I've heard that Muslims and Christians don't get along very well.

Isma'il: The Qur'an has many positive things to say about Christians. Good Muslims should respect Christians because they are followers of the Holy Books. Allah (swt) praised Christians.

Abdullah: Oh really, does the Qur'an say that?

Isma'il: Yes, there's an ayah that says,

> "... You will surely find **those closest in love to the believers** to be those who say, 'We are Christians.' This is because some of them are pastors and monks, and they are not proud." (Al-Maidah 5:82)

You know Abdullah, if we see this ayah, it means that these people are humble.

Abdullah: How can you say that Christians are humble? Is it because the ayah says they're not arrogant?

Isma'il: Yes, because if they're true followers of Isa al-Masih (as), then they have surrendered their life to Allah's (swt) power by having faith in Isa al-Masih (as) as a predestined Mercy from Allah (swt). Nowadays, there are many conceited people. They think they can get into paradise by their own effort and power or because of their background. They think that by doing good deeds, showing kindness to others, feeding the poor, fasting and performing sacrifices, and many other religious duties, they will get into paradise.

Abdullah: But there is nothing wrong with doing good things. Isn't doing good deeds a good thing?

Isma'il: I agree with you. Doing good things and helping people are great while we're in this world. But I believe **we can't** use those things to **bribe Allah** (swt) **for the purpose of getting into paradise**.

Abdullah: What do you mean? I'm not trying to bribe Allah (swt).

Isma'il: Well, if we do good deeds for the purpose of getting into paradise, it means we are using the good deeds as a kind of bribe so that Allah (swt) will let us into paradise. So why would Allah (swt) accept our good deeds when our motives are wrong? How can we expect Allah (swt) to accept these good deeds? And besides that, even if we do many good deeds, we also do many bad deeds. Think about it. We make a lot of mistakes, don't we?

Abdullah: Well, you got me there.

Isma'il: Even though we do many good deeds, we also make many mistakes every day. We're deceiving ourselves if we believe that we don't! Allah (swt) sees our good deeds, but He wants to deal with our mistakes and our shame.

Abdullah: But why can't our good deeds help us?

Isma'il: I'll tell you. Let me show you how the good deeds we do have no lasting value. Would you agree that good deeds won't help unbelievers to get into paradise?

Abdullah: Probably.

Isma'il: That's right. There's an ayah that says,

> **"The works of disbelievers** in their Lord **are like ashes** blown by the wind on a stormy day. They can do nothing against what they deserve. This is going far astray."
> (Ibrahim 14:18)

So, what about if someone thinks they're good and they think they're doing good deeds? Will their good deeds help them?

Abdullah: Sure. Why not?

Isma'il: Well, Abdullah, we could be wrong about whether our deeds are truly good or not. The Qur'an warns us,

"Say, 'Shall we tell you who will be the most lost in terms of deeds? It is those whose efforts go astray in this world. They think that they do good.'" (Al-Kahf 18:103-104)

Abdullah: Hmm, …

Isma'il: How can we be sure that our judgment is a reliable guide? **We might think that we're good, but we're not. We might think that we're doing good things when our deeds are actually worthless.**

Abdullah: But what if we do things that we know are good, like prayers? Certainly Allah (swt) will accept our prayers as something good, right?

Isma'il: Not necessarily. **Even our prayers might not qualify as something good.** It says in the Qur'an that,

"Human beings are as hasty to pray for things that are wrong as they pray for things that are good. The human being is often hasty." (Al-Isra 17:11[1])

Abdullah: But I still think that our good deeds will help us.

Isma'il: Abdullah, our misdeeds are a very serious thing. Our good deeds can never cover our impurities. No matter how many good things we do, our good deeds can never outweigh our bad deeds. Allah (swt) punishes people for the wicked things they do. The Qur'an says,

"If Allah were to punish people for their wickedness, he would not leave any living creature on it, but he gives them a specified lifespan. When their lifespan is up, they cannot postpone or advance it even one hour." (Al-Nahl 16:61)

Abdullah: What about sacrificing an animal? Can't that help us? I know that you sacrifice a sheep every year for Eid al-Adha. Do you believe that by sacrificing a sheep, its blood will cover your mistakes and satisfy Allah (swt)?

Isma'il: No, Abdullah, sacrificing animals can't benefit us either.

Abdullah: Then why do you do it every year?

Isma'il: My purpose in buying the animal is to give the meat to poor people. I want to help the poor people so they can have some meat to eat. You know how expensive meat is, and I'm sure there are many poor people who can't afford to buy meat. So I do this because I care about them.

Abdullah: So you perform the sacrifice to get a reward from Allah (swt)?

Isma'il: Not really, Abdullah. There's an ayah that talks about people sacrificing camels. It says,

"It is not their meat nor their blood, that reaches Allah: it is your piety that reaches Him: ..." (Al-Hajj 22:37[2])

Abdullah: Okay, even if our good deeds don't help us get into paradise when we die, maybe there's another way to get into paradise. Some people believe they will go to Hell first, but they will only have to stay there for a short time, and then they can get out.

Isma'il: How can they get out?

Abdullah: They believe that the good deeds they did in this life will help them. They also believe that if people pray for them after they die, they can get out faster.

Isma'il: Does the Qur'an say that?

Abdullah: I don't know, but that's what I've heard some people say.

Isma'il: You know, Abdullah, there are many Muslims who just believe what other people tell them. I hear them say things like, "Oh, my friend said this, my friends say that, or my Muslim teacher said this and that..." But we as Muslims should believe what it says in the Qur'an.

Abdullah: Yes, that's true. So, what does the Qur'an say then?

Isma'il: Well, according to what you've said, some people believe they will only have to stay in Hell for a short time. But the Qur'an says,

"Those who deny the truth and reject our revelations are **headed for hell, where they will be eternally**." (Al-Baqarah 2:39[1])

It means they will stay in Hell forever, and whatever good deeds they may have done can't help them!

Abdullah: I have a Muslim friend who usually prays for people when they die. My friend thinks that his prayers for the dead can help them to escape from the torment of Hell. What do you think, Isma'il?

Isma'il: I think it's better to see what it says in the Qur'an. There's an ayah that says,

"The followers will say: 'If only we had another chance, we would disown them [*their leaders*] just as they have disowned us.' **Thus God** [*Allah*] **will make them bitterly regret their works. They will not leave hell**." (Al-Baqarah 2:167[1])

In another ayah it says,

"Such people will have hell as their home, and they will have no way out." (Al-Nisa 4:121[1])

So it's important to notice that the **people in Hell won't get a second chance, and they won't be able to escape**. **They will only remember their deeds with regret.**

Abdullah: I never knew that before. I thought that our good deeds could help us to get out of Hell. Last week, I talked with my neighbors, and they said that they believe that the prophet Muhammad (pbuh) will save them from Hell.

Isma'il: As I told you, there are many Muslims who just believe what other people tell them. As Muslims, we're supposed to believe what it says in the Qur'an. In the Qur'an, **the prophet Muhammad** (pbuh) **is** often **called a warner**. According to the Qur'an, Muhammad (pbuh) was commanded by Allah (swt) to refer to himself that way. It says,

"Say, 'I cannot help or harm myself except as Allah wills. If I knew the unseen, I would make great use of the good, and evil would not touch me. **I am only a warner** and bearer of good news for believing people.'" (Al-Aaraf 7:188)

There's also another ayah that says,

"We truly sent you as a bearer of good news and a warner. **You are not responsible for those headed to hell**." (Al-Baqarah 2:119)

This ayah means that the prophet Muhammad (pbuh) doesn't have any responsibility for helping people who are in Hell, and is of no benefit to them.

Abdullah: Hmm, but if I told that to our neighbors, they would probably be angry!

Isma'il: Angry? I'm sure they wouldn't be angry if they knew that the Qur'an said this. Besides, **it's not my opinion. This is what Allah** (swt) **said** to the prophet Muhammad (pbuh). Please notice the word "WE." It means Allah (swt). So, in this ayah, Allah (swt) was speaking to the prophet Muhammad (pbuh), right?

Abdullah: Yes, I guess you're right, …

Isma'il: Anyway, suppose the neighbors were angry, then it means they're angry with Allah (swt), and they don't agree with what it says in the Qur'an.

Abdullah: So Isma'il, why do some Muslims believe that if they die while committing Jihad, they'll go straight to paradise?

Isma'il: Well, Abdullah, according to your opinion, what is the meaning of Jihad?

Abdullah: Jihad means to fight a war against infidels.

Isma'il: And do you know the meaning of the infidels?

Abdullah: Infidels are idolaters and people who don't believe in Allah (swt).

Isma'il: You're right, Abdullah. It means unbelievers. And do you know who the unbelievers are?

Abdullah: Well, I know that some Muslims believe that Jews and Christians are infidels. What do you think?

Isma'il: According to the Qur'an, the disciples of Isa al-Masih (as) called themselves **Muslims**.

"… The disciples [*hawariyun*] said, 'We are Allah's helpers. We have believed in Allah, so **testify that we have submitted** [*are Muslims*].'" (Aal Imran 3:52)

So how can the followers of Isa al-Masih (as) be called infidels?

Abdullah: Well some people think the followers of Isa worship three gods, so that would make them infidels.

Isma'il: But the Qur'an says the followers of Isa (as) worship the same god as we do.

Abdullah: Really?

Isma'il: Yes. The Qur'an says,

"Do not argue with the people of the book but [speak] in a fair manner, except with the wicked among them. Say, 'We believe in what was revealed to us and what was revealed to you. Our god and your god is one, and we submit to him.'" (Al-Ankabut 29:46)

Since they're believers in one god, how can we say that they worship three gods?

Abdullah: I don't know.

Isma'il: Anyway, I don't understand how they can think that the followers of Isa are infidels. The Qur'an says that **Allah** (swt) **distinguishes the followers of Isa al-Masih** (as) **from the infidels**. In fact, **Allah** (swt) **exalts the followers of Isa** (as) **far above the infidel unbelievers**. In the Qur'an it says,

"**Allah said**, 'Isa, **I will** make you die and raise you up to me, and purify you from the disbelievers, and **make your followers higher than the disbelievers** until the day of resurrection. …" (Aal Imran 3:55)

Abdullah: Hmm, I guess I never thought about it like that before.

Isma'il: Believers and infidels are opposites. Allah (swt) said the followers of Isa al-Masih (as) are believers, not disbelieving infidels.

Abdullah: In that case, what would happen to a Muslim who killed a follower of Isa (as) but thought that he was killing an infidel?

Isma'il: Well, the Qur'an tells us about what will happen to someone who kills a believer. There's an ayah that says,

"He who kills a believer intentionally will be punished in hell forever. Allah is angry with him and has damned him and prepared great torment for him." (Al-Nisa 4:93)

Abdullah: But what if the person didn't realize they were killing a believer?

Isma'il: In that case, he still killed someone wrongfully. And according to the Qur'an, even though it was a mistake, he will still have to pay the penalty for killing the person. It says,

"A believer should never kill another believer, but mistakes happen. If someone kills a believer by mistake, he must free one believing slave and pay compensation to the victim's relatives, unless they willingly forgo compensation. If the victim is a believer, but belonged to a community with which you are at war, then the compensation is only to free a believing slave; whereas, if the person killed belonged to a community with whom you have a treaty, then the compensation should be paid to the relatives in addition to freeing a believing slave. Anyone who does not have the means to do this must fast for two consecutive months. Allah ordains this atonement. Allah is All-Knowing, All-Wise." (Al-Nisa 4:92[1])

Anyway, did you know that there's an ayah that says that Jihad doesn't guarantee that a person will get into paradise?

Abdullah: What?! Are you sure?

Isma'il: Yes. The ayah says,

"Did you think that ye [*you*] would enter Heaven [*Paradise*] without Allah testing those of you who fought hard (in His Cause) and remained steadfast." (Aal Imran 3:142[2])

Abdullah: I've heard that there are some ayat that talk about killing people. Like, kill that man because he's bad. Or, kill those men because they're infidels. What do you think?

Isma'il: Well Abdullah, let's look at several of the ayat that have been used to justify wrongfully killing people in the name of Allah (swt). One ayah says,

"… kill the polytheists wherever you find them. …" (Al-Tawbah 9:5[3])

Another ayah they use says,

"If you find disbelievers, strike their necks. …" (Muhammad 47:4)

The problem is that only part of the ayah is quoted. Or even if the entire ayah is quoted, it's done without considering the context and the ayat surrounding them. Well, if we're going to take the ayat literally like that, we'll have to start by killing ourselves first.

Abdullah: What do you mean?

Isma'il: We all make mistakes and go astray, right? We all have doubt and unbelief in our hearts sometimes. And sometimes we set up idols in our hearts by making other things more important than Allah (swt), right? So if an infidel is an unbeliever or someone who loves pleasure or self, then sometimes we are infidels too. But instead of killing other people,

I think it's better if we kill the sin, unbelief, and love of the world in ourselves. Otherwise, we will end up like the people it talks about in Al-Isra 17:18, where it says,

"As for anyone who prefers this momentary life, We readily grant whatever We will to whomever We will. Then We condemn him to the suffering of hell which he will have to endure, disgraced and disowned!" (Al-Isra 17:18[1])

Abdullah: Oh, no! But suppose you have a friend who doesn't believe in Allah (swt). What would you do then, Isma'il?

Isma'il: I would pray for them. I would pray for them to turn and believe in Allah (swt). I would also pray that they would come to know **the Mercy and Forgiveness of Allah (swt) in Isa al-Masih** (as) and that they would become his [Isa's] (as) followers. There's an ayah that says,

"Tell believers to forgive those who do not hope for Allah's days, when he will reward people as they deserve." (Al-Jathiyah 45:14)

Abdullah: So why would you pray for them to become followers of Isa al-Masih (as)?

Isma'il: Why not? Allah has promised many fantastic things to the followers of Isa al-Masih (as).

Abdullah: Really? Like what?

Isma'il: I'll tell you. Here's an example from the Qur'an that shows some of Allah's (swt) promises to Isa's (as) followers. It says,

"Allah said, '**Isa, I will** make you die and raise you up to me, and purify you from the disbelievers, and **make your followers higher than the disbelievers** until the day of resurrection. ...'" (Aal Imran 3:55)

Abdullah: It's very interesting that it says that the followers of Isa al-Masih (as) were superior because Allah (swt) placed them above the unbelievers. But I think Allah (swt) said that about the followers of Isa during Isa's (as) lifetime, not about his followers today.

Isma'il: How can that be, Abdullah? Please notice the words "until the Day of Resurrection." **The Day of Resurrection hasn't happened yet**, right? So it means that Allah's (swt) promise is for whoever follows Isa (as) today too. And do you know what happens to the unbelievers? I mean those people who don't want to believe in and follow Isa (as)?

Abdullah: I'm not sure.

Isma'il: Well, the next ayah goes on to tell us. It says,

"But I will severely punish the unbelievers both in this world and the hereafter, and they will have no one to help them." (Aal Imran 3:56[1])

So, Abdullah, in the first ayah, Allah (swt) promised something wonderful to the follower of Isa (as), but in the second ayah, Allah (swt) promised something horrible to those who don't believe in, obey or follow Isa (as). So, I'm not surprised if Allah (swt) always helps me to solve my problems in this world, because I have faith in Allah (swt), and I follow Isa (as) based on what's promised in the first ayah. And **I** also **believe that Allah** (swt) **will help me in the world to come**, not because I'm a good person or a bad person but because **Allah** (swt) **has promised to help whoever believes in Isa al-Masih** (as) in this world and the next. That's why **I believe in Allah** (swt) **and trust His promises**!

Abdullah: I'd be interested in hearing more about Isa al-Masih (as), but I have to leave now. I'm sorry, Isma'il.

Isma'il: That's okay Abdullah. I have to go now too. I need to go to the post office to check my P.O. Box. What do you have going on?

Abdullah: I have to go to the repair shop to get my motorcycle fixed.

Isma'il: Oh, I see. By the way, if you have time, try to go to the bookshop and find some helpful books on the Qur'an. And please don't forget to look for the ayat about Isa al-Masih (as) in the Qur'an. Then when we meet again, we can look at the ayat together. I'll see you later. Assalamu'alaikum.

Abdullah: Wa'alaikum salam wa-rahmatullah wa-barakatuh.

❖ ೕೂೕೂೕೂೕೂೕೂೕೂ ❖

Chapter 2: The List

A few days after our previous conversation, Abdullah and I met again. It was Friday, so we went to the Mosque for the Zuhr (noon) prayers. Afterward, we went to a café for lunch. I didn't have to go back to work that afternoon, so we sat around and talked for a while.

Isma'il: So Abdullah. How's your motorcycle?

Abdullah: Well, I need to buy new brakes for my motorcycle.

Isma'il: So what's wrong with the brakes?

Abdullah: You know my motorcycle is getting old. The brakes just need to be replaced. It's to be expected.

Isma'il: Oh, I see. Anyway, did you find any books to help you with understanding the Qur'an yet?

Abdullah: Alhamdulillah, I did. I just bought a Qur'an with tafsir (commentary). It's quite beautiful and ornate. It's embossed in gold. I'll show it to you the next time you come over to my house.

Isma'il: That's great! I look forward to seeing it.

Abdullah: So Isma'il, here's my note. I wrote down a few ayat (verses) that I found about Isa al-Masih (as), but I didn't have time to finish.

Isma'il: That's okay. Tell me, which ayat (verses) did you find?

Abdullah: I'm sorry, but I was busy the past few days. So I actually only got through Surah 2. Anyway, here are the ayat I found about Isa al-Masih (as): Al-Baqarah 2:87, 2:136, and 2:253.

Isma'il: It's too bad you didn't have time to find more, but that's okay, we can look at them together some other time.

Abdullah: I promise, I'll look for more ayat later.

Isma'il: I started to make a list of ayat about Isa al-Masih (as) too. Why don't you take my list with you? That way, you can take a look at it, and then we can discuss it later.

Here's the list I gave to Abdullah:

<u>AYAT (VERSES) ABOUT ISA AL-MASIH</u>

Qur'an

Isa al-Masih is the son of Maryam: Surah 2:87, 253; 3:45; 4:157, 171; 5:17 (2x), 46, 72, 75, 78, 110, 112, 114, 116; 9:31; 19:34; 23:50; 33:7; 43:57; 57:24; 61:6, 14

Isa al-Masih is the Messiah (al-Masih): Surah 3:45; 4:157, 171, 172; 5:17 (2x), 72 (2x), 75; 9:30, 31

Isa al-Masih is a Messenger/Apostle of Allah: Surah 2:253; 3:53; 4:157, 171; 5:75

Isa al-Masih is the Servant of Allah: Surah 4:172; 19:30; 43:59

Isa al-Masih is a sign (for all people): Surah 19:21, 21:91; 23:50

Isa al-Masih is the Word of Allah: Surah 3:45; 4:171

Isa al-Masih is righteous: Surah 3:46; 6:85

Isa al-Masih is a witness: Surah 4:159; 5:117

Isa al-Masih is blessed/a blessing: Surah 19:31; 43:59

Isa al-Masih is a proverb: Surah 43:57, 59

Isa al-Masih is a preferred messenger: Surah 2:253

Isa al-Masih was raised in degree: Surah 2:253

Isa al-Masih is great (highly exalted):   Surah 3:45

Isa al-Masih was brought near to Allah: Surah 3:45

Isa al-Masih is a Spirit from Allah: Surah 4:171

Isa al-Masih is a gift: Surah 19:19

Isa al-Masih is sinless/holy: Surah 19:19

Isa al-Masih is a predestined mercy from Allah: Surah 19:21

Isa al-Masih is a prophet: Surah 19:30

Isa al-Masih was a prophet from birth: Surah 19:30

Isa al-Masih is the Word of Truth: Surah 19:34

Isa al-Masih was spoken to by Allah: Surah 2:253; 3:55; 5:110, 115, 116; 42:13

Isa al-Masih did miracles: Surah 2:87, 253; 3:49; 43:63; 61:6

Isa al-Masih was born of a virgin: Surah 3:47; 19:19-22; 21:91; 66:12

Isa al-Masih was aided by the Holy Spirit: Surah 2:87, 253; 5:110

Isa al-Masih was taught by Allah: 3:48; 5:110

Isa al-Masih knows hidden things: 3:49; 52

Isa al-Masih created/gave life by Allah's permission:Surah 3:49; 5:110

Isa al-Masih gives life: Surah 3:49; 5:110

Isa al-Masih healed people: Surah 3:49; 5:110

Isa al-Masih raised the dead: Surah 3:49; 5:110

Isa al-Masih confirmed the Tawrah: Surah 3:50; 5:46

Isa al-Masih is to be obeyed in order to be on the straight path: Surah 3:50-51; 43:63-64

Isa al-Masih ascended to heaven after his death and resurrection: Surah 3:55; 4:158

Isa al-Masih spoke as a baby: Surah 5:110; 19:28-33

Isa al-Masih came with a sign from Allah:
                                Surah 3:49-50

Isa al-Masih guides people to the truth: Surah 3:49

Isa al-Masih died by the will of Allah: Surah 3:55

Isa al-Masih is to be followed: Surah 3:55

Isa al-Masih was inspired by Allah: Surah 4:163

Isa al-Masih was protected by Allah: Surah 5:110

Isa al-Masih provided food from heaven:
                                Surah 5:112-115

Isa al-Masih is alive with Allah: Surah 5:117

Isa al-Masih only spoke what Allah told him to say:
                                Surah 5:117

Isa al-Masih was given refuge by Allah: Surah 23:50

Isa al-Masih had a strong covenant with Allah: Surah 33:7
Isa al-Masih was given commands by Allah: Surah 42:13

Isa al-Masih knows the future: Surah 43:61

Isa al-Masih is coming back: Surah 43:61

Isa al-Masih is to be obeyed: Surah 43:63

Abdullah: Your list is awesome.

Isma'il: Thanks, Abdullah. Anyway, that's what I came up with.

Abdullah: My list is so short compared with yours.

Isma'il: That's ok, Abdullah. A long time ago, I didn't know the ayat about Isa al-Masih (as) either. I learned little by little, and finally, I found more than 90 ayat about Isa al-Masih (as) in the Qur'an.

Abdullah: By the way, when I was at the bookshop buying the Qur'an, I met Akbar.

Isma'il: Akbar? Which Akbar?

Abdullah: Akbar, who was our friend when we were in high school. He was a leader in our class. Do you remember him?

Isma'il: Yes, I remember Akbar. He was a nice guy.

Abdullah: When I met Akbar, he asked me why I was buying a Qur'an. I told him that you asked me to find all the ayat about Isa al-Masih in the Qur'an and that you thought it would be helpful if I read some tafsir on those ayat in the Qur'an. I had a short talk with him. He mentioned several things about the life of Isa al-Masih too.

Isma'il: So what did he say?

Abdullah: He said if I wanted to know more about the life of Isa al-Masih, why don't I just buy an Injil and read about Isa's life in it?

Isma'il: Really? Did he say that?

Abdullah: Yes, but I wouldn't want to do that. I've heard that the Injil can't be trusted because it's been corrupted. So we can't know which parts are true and which parts have been changed.

Isma'il: So how's Akbar doing these days?

Abdullah: From what he said, it sounds like everything is going well for him.

Isma'il: I remember how the three of us always had a study group together at home the day before we took our exams. During Ramadan, I always visited his house at night for the Iftar meal. It was fun. But I haven't seen him for quite a while. I'd like to see him again sometime. But I don't know where he lives now, do you?

Abdullah: No. I'm not sure. I didn't ask for his address.

Isma'il: That's too bad.

Abdullah: Anyway, Isma'il, you don't have an Injil, do you?

Isma'il: Yes, I do. I have an Injil. And I've even read it.

Abdullah: What?! You've read the Injil?

Isma'il: Why not? You know that I have a hobby of reading the autobiographies of famous people like great leaders, writers, movie stars and musicians. When I want to know about the life of someone, I always go to the bookstore and buy a book about them and read it. The Injil tells the stories of Yahya (as) and Isa (as), and their families, and about the Hawariyun (disciples) of Isa (as).

Abdullah: But the Injil is only for Christians, and besides that, many people have told me that the Injil has many things in it that aren't true.

Isma'il: I don't think so, Abdullah. I've read the Injil, and I didn't find anything bad in the stories about Yahya (as) or Isa al-Masih (as). Besides that, the Qur'an says **the Injil contains guidance and light**. (Al-Maidah 5:46) I always want to be guided and enlightened by the word of Allah (swt), so it's good to read the Injil.

Abdullah: But I've heard that the Injil has been corrupted.

Isma'il: It's too bad if people think the Injil has been corrupted. I hope you're not someone who feels the Injil has been changed, because **anyone who thinks that the Injil has been corrupted insults Allah** (swt).

Abdullah: Insults Allah (swt)? How can you say that?

Isma'il: You know that Allah (swt) revealed His words to many prophets a long time ago. If we think the Injil has been corrupted, it means we think Allah (swt) is weak. Do you think Allah (swt) is so weak that He couldn't guard His own words after He revealed them?

Abdullah: Of course not. But what would stop people from changing the words in the Injil?

Isma'il: I don't think Allah (swt) will let people change His words. In the Qur'an, it says,

> "If all the trees on earth were pens, and the sea and seven more seas beside were ink, the words of Allah would not end, for **Allah is Almighty, Wise**." (Luqman 31:27[4])

This ayah (verse) says that because **Allah** (swt) **is mighty, He is powerful enough to guard and protect His words**.

Abdullah: I'm not sure I follow what you're saying.

Isma'il: The Qur'an repeatedly says that no one can change His words. One ayah says,

"Recite what has been revealed to you from your Lord's Book. **No one can change His words**, and you will never find any refuge except with Him." (Al-Kahf 18:27[1])

In another place, it says,

"(For) those who believe and are ever mindful of God [*Allah*], there is good news in the life of this world and the life to come. **There is no changing the words of God [*Allah*]**; this is truly the supreme triumph." (Yunus 10:63-64[1])

And another ayah says,

"Your Lord's word has been fulfilled in truth and justice. **There is no power that could change His words**. He is the All-Hearing, the All-Knowing." (Al-Anaam 6:115[1])

Abdullah: Have you read the Injil very often?

Isma'il: Yes. I read both the Qur'an and the Injil. Besides, it's not wrong for me to read the Injil. The Injil is a good book. It talks a lot about the compassion and mercy of Allah (swt) for us. The Qur'an shows us why we need to read the Injil. In one place, it says,

"And he revealed the book to you in truth, confirming what is in his possession and **he revealed the Tawrah and the Injil beforehand as guidance to people**, and he revealed the criterion. Disbelievers in Allah's signs will have severe torment. Allah is strong and avenging." (Aal Imran 3:3-4)

So, we see that the Tawrah and the Injil are guidance for all people. Later it says,

"**We made Isa** son of Mariam follow in their footsteps, **confirming the Tawrah in his possession, and we gave him the Injil, in which is guidance and light, confirming the Tawrah in his possession, as guidance and an admonition to the reverent**." (Al-Maidah 5:46)

Wouldn't you agree that we all need guidance and light?

Abdullah: Yes, but I thought the Tawrah and the Injil were only for Jews and Christians.

Isma'il: No, Abdullah. The Tawrah and the Injil are for everyone. Remember when it says that **the Tawrah and the Injil are** "**guidance to people**," it means **for all people**.

Abdullah: But it still seems strange to me if a good Muslim like you reads the Injil.

Isma'il: I don't think it's strange for a Muslim to read the Injil. I believe that the prophet Muhammad (pbuh) knew that the Injil was good for us to read.

Abdullah: How do you know?

Isma'il: Because the Qur'an says that the **Injil is guidance and light, it confirms the previous scriptures, and it enlightens the righteous**. Think about it, Allah (swt) revealed to the prophet Muhammad (pbuh) that the Injil contains guidance and light.

Abdullah: Well, just because he knew about the Injil doesn't necessarily mean he wanted us to read it.

Isma'il: I believe that if Allah (swt) didn't want us to read the Injil, then He wouldn't have revealed those things to the prophet Muhammad (pbuh), but he did. We are even encouraged as Muslims to read the Injil. According to the Qur'an, this is what Allah (swt) told him to say,

"People of the book, you have no foundation unless you uphold the Tawrah and Injil and what was revealed to you by your Lord. ..." (Al-Maidah 5:68)

As I told you, Abdullah, I like reading autobiographies of famous people. In the Tawrah and Injil, I enjoy reading the experiences of the godly people who followed Allah (swt). It's such a blessing for me. I also like reading the Zabur.

Abdullah: Dawud's (as) book the Zabur?

Isma'il: Yes. The Zabur came from Allah (swt) too. Remember what it says in the Qur'an,

"Your Lord knows everyone in the heavens and the earth. We preferred some prophets above others, and we brought Dawud the Zabur" (Al-Isra 17:55)

It also says,

"We have written in the Zabur after the reminder, 'My righteous servants will inherit the earth.'" (Al-Anbiya 21:105)

Abdullah: Some Muslims believe that all of the Tawrah, Zabur, and Injil are in the Qur'an. What do you think, Isma'il?

Isma'il: I've read the Tawrah, Zabur, and Injil. I've found a number of references and allusions to the stories and teaching of the Tawrah, Zabur, and Injil in the Qur'an too. Allah (swt) repeatedly said in the Qur'an to "remember" or "remember when" to refer to events and teaching in the Tawrah, Zabur, and Injil.

Abdullah: Really? Can you show me?

Isma'il: Sure. But first, you have to know the meaning of the word **Injil**. Do you know what it is, Abdullah?

Abdullah: I think, it was the book that contained the message that Allah (swt) gave to Isa al-Masih (as)?

Isma'il: Yes, the teaching of Isa al-Masih (as) is in the Injil, but there's a lot more to it than that, Abdullah. **The real meaning of Injil is "the good news."** The good news is the message about Isa al-Masih (as) and what Allah (swt) has done for us through him (Isa (as)). It's the message that Allah (swt) sent Isa al-Masih (as) to die and rise again so we too could have peace, and have victory over Satan, and be exalted to Paradise after we die. That's the meaning of the Injil! And all of this is found in the Qur'an. According to the Qur'an Isa (as) said,

"Peace be upon me the day I was born, the day I will die, and the day I will be resurrected alive!" (Mariam 19:33)

Consider this: no one can say 'peace be upon me' unless they have the authority to pronounce peace. Besides having peace because of Isa al-Masih (as), Allah (swt) promised that the followers of Isa would have victory over Satan. In the Quran, it says,

"... **We [*Allah*] aided the believers [in Isa] against their enemy, and they were victorious**." (Al-Saff 61:14)

In another ayah, Allah (swt) also promised to exalt the followers of Isa (as), it says,

"Allah said, 'Isa, I will make you die and raise you up to me, and purify you from the disbelievers, and **make your followers higher than the disbelievers** until the day of resurrection. ...'" (Aal Imran 3:55)

So that's the message of the Injil. It means the good news about how Allah (swt) has provided the Way for us to be made pure, and to have peace and blessings in this life, and to receive mercy on the Day of Judgment, and to enter into paradise.

Abdullah: Allah's (swt) way for us? I don't understand. How are the ayat related to all of that?

Isma'il: Think about the words "**I will exalt those who follow you**." Who is it talking about?

Abdullah: The followers of Isa al-Masih (as)?

Isma'il: That's right. And it says that Allah (swt) exalts them, but exalts them where?

Abdullah: Above the unbelievers?

Isma'il: Yes, but Allah (swt) did three things first. The first thing was that Allah (swt) caused Isa (as) to die, then Allah (swt) raised Isa (as) to Himself, and the final thing was that Allah (swt) made Isa (as) victorious, not just over unbelievers but also over death. Because of this, those who believe and follow Isa al-Masih (as) will also be victorious over death and will enter into paradise.

Abdullah: Enter into paradise? How do you know they get into paradise?

Isma'il: Well, the ayah goes on to say,

"Then you will return to me…" (Aal Imran 3:55)

So, based on this ayah, where are the followers of Isa al-Masih (as) going?

Abdullah: They're returning to Allah (swt), I guess.

Isma'il: That's right. And where do you think Allah is (swt)?

Abdullah: In heaven, … Allah (swt) is in heaven.

Isma'il: Yes, Allah (swt) is in heaven. Allah (swt) is referred to as "He Who is in heaven" (Al-Mulk 67:16, 17[2,3]).

Abdullah: You know, Isma'il, I've been thinking about your life. I can see how much you care about people.

Isma'il: Alhamdulillah. Thanks for the compliment, Abdullah. It's nice that you think that, but you should remember that Allah (swt) loves us. The Qur'an says,

"He [*Allah*] is forgiving and loving." (Al-Buruj 85:14)

That's why I love people; it's because Allah (swt) has loved me first. Anyway, what made you say that I love and care about people?

Abdullah: Because of your prayers for people. Two weeks ago, you took me to visit our neighbor. He had been very sick for months, and you prayed for him. I saw him the next morning, and he was healed! You had me wait in the other room while you prayed for him. What were you praying?

Isma'il: When I pray, I'm praying to Allah (swt). I'm not praying because I want other people to see or hear me. I pray because I believe that Allah (swt) will hear and answer my prayers. As the Qur'an says,

"Pray to your Lord in supplication and in secret. …" (Al-Aaraf 7:55)

Abdullah: You know, I was quite surprised that our neighbor was healed! What did you say when you prayed?

Isma'il: Whenever I pray for someone who's sick, I always remember how Isa al-Masih (as) performed many miracles, and one of his miracles was to heal sick people. So in the case of our neighbor, I simply called on Isa al-Masih (as) and asked him to heal our neighbor. There's an ayah that says Isa (as) would be,

"… a messenger to the people of Israel, [*saying*,] 'I have brought you a sign from your Lord: I create a bird for you from clay and I breathe into it and it will be a [living] bird by Allah's permission. **I heal the man born blind and the leper and give life**

to the dead by Allah's permission. I tell you what you eat and what you store in your houses. That is truly **a sign for you, if you believe**.'" (Aal Imran 3:49)

Abdullah: So why do you think about the miracles of Isa (as) al-Masih?

Isma'il: Because Allah (swt) has given Isa (as) the authority and permission to heal. And besides that, Isa (as) is near stationed to Allah (swt). As we're told in the Qur'an,

"When the angels said, 'Mariam, Allah gives you good news of a word from him, whose name will be the Messiah [*al-Masih*], **Isa**, son of Mariam; **highly exalted in this world and the hereafter, brought near [to Allah]**.'" (Aal Imran 3:45)

Since Isa (as) is near-stationed to Allah (swt) and Allah (swt) has given Isa (as) authority and permission to heal, I can pray to Allah (swt) and ask Allah (swt) to heal someone based on the authority that He has given to Isa al-Masih (as).

Abdullah: I'm not sure that I understand. I know that Isa (as) healed people in the past, but how can we pray based on the authority that Allah (swt) gave to Isa?

Isma'il: You don't need to understand everything, but we're supposed to trust Allah (swt) with what we do know and understand. We're not told to rely on our understanding when we pray, we're told to believe. Remember the words,

"**That is truly a sign for you, if you believe**." (Aal Imran 3:49)

I believed that Allah (swt) would heal our neighbor by the authority that He has given to Isa, and the result was that our neighbor was healed! There's the proof! I remember reading al-Ghazali's story about a blind man who was healed by Isa (as). I'm sure the blind man didn't understand how he was going to be healed. He just believed that Allah (swt) would heal him. So when Isa (as) said to the blind man, "Give me your hand," the blind man believed and stretched out his hand, and Allah (swt) healed him.[6]

Abdullah: That's interesting.

Isma'il: What's interesting?

Abdullah: Well, the man that Isa (as) healed was born blind. Why do you think Isa (as) healed someone who was born blind instead of someone who became blind when they were older?

Isma'il: I don't know, but it reminds me of how since Adam (as) and his wife Hawa disobeyed Allah (swt), we are all born blind spiritually.

Abdullah: Blind spiritually?

Isma'il: Yes, you can see it in the story of Adam (as) and his wife Hawa. After Adam (as) and Hawa disobeyed Allah (swt), they were kicked out of Paradise. Taha 20:125-126 says,

"He [*Adam*] will say, 'My Lord, why have you raised me blind whereas I was able to see before?' (*Allah*) will say, 'Just as Our Signs came to you and you forgot them, in the same way, you too will this Day be forgotten.'" (Taha 20:125-126[1])

Abdullah: Maybe it just means that Adam (as) became physically blind.

Isma'il: No, Abdullah, it has to mean spiritually blind because the story goes on to tell us that this is the consequence for all transgressors. It says,

"This is how we repay him who goes too far and does not believe in the signs of his Lord. And the punishment in the Hereafter is more severe and most enduring." (Taha 20:127[1])

If it meant physically blind, then we would all have to be physically blind since we all make many mistakes, right? So it must mean blind in our hearts, Abdullah.

There's an ayah that says,

"Have they not traveled through the land, so that their hearts gain wisdom and their ears learn to listen? **For it is not the eyes that are blind**, **but the hearts** within the breasts." (Al-Hajj 22:46[1])

Do you know what happens to people who are spiritually blind in their hearts?

Abdullah: I'm not sure.

Isma'il: In the Qur'an, it says,

"For whoever (refuses to see, and so) is blind in this world, will also be blind in the life to come, and still farther astray from the (straight) path." (Al-Isra 17:72[1])

Abdullah: Oh no! It would be horrible if we were blind in the hereafter. But what can we do so we won't be blind spiritually?

Isma'il: In the Qur'an, Isa al-Masih (as) said,

"…I heal the man born blind,…" (Aal Imran 3:49)

And later Allah (swt) said to Isa al-Masih (as),

"… you healed the one born blind…" (Al-Maidah 5:110)

So, Abdullah, it means that we have to believe in Isa al-Masih (as) as someone who is able to heal our spiritual blindness.

Abdullah: I have a book called "Tales of the Prophets"[7]. I read that **only Isa al-Masih** (as) **performed many extraordinary miracles**.

Isma'il: Like what?

Abdullah: Like **giving life to a clay bird and bringing dead people back to life.**

Isma'il: I believe that Isa's (as) miracles show us that **Isa (as) is a life-giver. He can give physical life and spiritual life.**

Abdullah: What do you mean?

Isma'il: According to the Qur'an, when Allah (swt) created man, Allah (swt) breathed into Adam (as) with His Spirit, and man became a living being with hearing, sight, and feeling. The Qur'an says,

"Then he [*Allah*] formed him and breathed into him of his spirit, and he gave you hearing, sight and hearts. How little you give thanks!" (Al-Sajdah 32:9)

So, we can see how Allah's (swt) Spirit has the special power to give life. Since Isa (as) is called a spirit from Him in the Qur'an (Al-Nisa 4:171), it means his breath has the power to give life, so the clay bird became a living bird, and the dead came back to life.

Abdullah: I think he actually healed people and raised dead people to life, but do you believe the ayat really mean that Isa can give spiritual life?

Isma'il: Yes, Abdullah, the ayat in Qur'an mean both; **Isa (as) actually raises dead people back to life, and he gives life to people who are spiritually dead.** I'm reminded of several sayings about this by a couple of Muslim authors. One of them said,

"With one breath you bring back to life
a hundred dead souls -
Who are you, O Christ [*al-Masih*]?
The Spirit of God?
Or the Water of Life?"[8]

Another one wrote,

"I called through your door,
'Spiritual people are gathering in the street. Come out!'
'Leave me alone; I'm sick,' (You said)
'I don't care if you're dead! (I said)
Isa is here, and he wants to resurrect someone!'"[9]

Abdullah: I feel dead in my spirit. Do you think that Isa (as) can help me?

Isma'il: Yes, He can. Isa (as) can give you spiritual life and peace.

Abdullah: Really? How?

Isma'il: Let me tell you, ...

Abdullah: Oh, wait, I just noticed the time.

Isma'il: Yes, it's getting late. When you have time, we can talk about it more then. I'd like to continue our conversation, but I have a few things I need to do before the Maghrib (evening) prayers, so I'd better go now. Are you going back to the mosque this evening?

Abdullah: No. I think I'll pray at home with my family. Anyway, I need to go too. You know I still have to check on my motorcycle to see if it's been fixed yet.

Isma'il: Ok, I'll see you later.

Abdullah: Oh, by the way, Isma'il, please don't forget our appointment next weekend. You're still planning on coming with my family and me to the zoo, right?

Isma'il: Yes, I'll be there. I won't forget,

Abdullah: Great! And please bring your selfie stick and tripod too. I want us to take lots of pictures.

Isma'il: That's a good idea. I'll bring them. Assalamu'alaikum.

Abdullah: Wa'alaikum salam wa-rahmatullah wa-barakatuh.

✤ 𑀰𑀓𑀰𑀓𑀰𑀓𑀰𑀓𑀰𑀓𑀰𑀓 ✤

Chapter 3: Breakfast

Abdullah called me early in the morning on the day we were going to the zoo. He asked me if I could come to his house for breakfast before we went to the zoo. While having breakfast, Abdullah asked me some questions about the love of Allah (swt) shown by sending Isa al-Masih (as).

Isma'il: This is a great day to go to the zoo. The weather is very nice today, Alhamdulillah.

Abdullah: That's good, because the last time I went to the zoo, it was cloudy and started to rain.

Isma'il: How is your motorcycle?

Abdullah: My motorcycle is fixed, and I finally got it back from the repair shop. It was inconvenient to get around not having my motorcycle, but it's okay now.

Isma'il: Alhamdulillah.

Abdullah: How's your work?

Isma'il: Okay, but I had a bit of a problem with my computer. You know that my neighbor borrowed my laptop. It turned out that he had opened an email from a source he didn't recognize, and it gave my laptop a virus. It almost destroyed my laptop. Alhamdulillah, I was able to fix everything. I ran a virus scan and cleaned up my laptop. I also ended up restoring a few files from my USB drives.

Abdullah: Were you angry with him?

Isma'il: Why should I be angry? He apologized, and besides that, I was able to fix the laptop.

Abdullah: Yes, but you still had to spend time fixing it. Anyway, it seems so easy for you to forgive the person who almost destroyed your laptop.

Isma'il: Abdullah, **Allah** (swt) **has forgiven me** and enlightened my heart to know His Mercy through Isa al-Masih (as). Since Allah (swt) has forgiven me, why shouldn't I forgive my friend's mistakes too?

Abdullah: It usually seems hard for me to forgive other people. Maybe it's easy for you because you are so close to Allah (swt).

Isma'il: Yes, alhamdulillah, I feel that Allah (swt) is close to me, and I want to be close to Allah (swt). Allah (swt) is like a close friend to me.

Abdullah: How can you be close to Allah (swt) like a friend? I've never heard before that Allah (swt) could be our friend.

Isma'il: It's true, that we can be friends with Allah (swt). The Qur'an even gives us an example of someone who was friends with Allah (swt). It tells us that Allah (swt) chose Ibrahim (as) to be a close friend. The Qur'an says,

"Who could be better in faith than those who submit themselves to God [*Allah*], and do good, and follow the faith of Abraham [*Ibrahim*], who turned away from all that is false? God [*Allah*] took Abraham [*Ibrahim*] as a friend." (Al-Nisa 4:125[1])

So I believe that Allah (swt) is my friend too. I believe that Allah (swt) knows me well, and I want to know Allah (swt) too.

Abdullah: Allah (swt) seems very far away to me. How can you truly know Allah (swt) when Allah (swt) is so far away?

Isma'il: Allah (swt) isn't far away, Abdullah. **Allah** (swt) **is near to us**. In the Qur'an it says,

"We created man and know what his soul whispers to him. **We are nearer to him than his jugular vein**." (Qaf 50:16)

Allah (swt) **is near to us**, and He is waiting for us to hear His call and turn to Him. In another ayah (verse), it says,

"If my worshipers ask you about Me, **I am near**, answering the prayer of the one who prays to Me. They should respond to Me and believe in Me in order to be guided.'" (Al-Baqarah 2:186[1])

So, even though Allah (swt) is near to us, we cannot come near to Him, because **He is holy and pure, but we are impious and impure**. There's an ayah that I told you about before that says,

"**Whoever comes to his Lord as an evildoer is destined for Hell** where he will neither die nor live." (Taha 20:74[1])

So, Abdullah, how can we come to Allah (swt) when we are evildoers?

Abdullah: I don't know.

Isma'il: What **we need** is **an intercessor or mediator, someone who is holy and pure and near to Allah** (swt) already, **who can go to Allah** (swt) **on our behalf**. And the only person like that is Isa al-Masih (as). Not only is **Isa** (as) someone who **is holy and pure, he is** also **near stationed to Allah** (swt). The Qur'an tells us that Isa (as) is near to Allah (swt) already.

"When the angels said, 'Mariam, Allah gives you good news of a word from him, whose name will be the Messiah, **Isa** son of Mariam, **highly exalted in this world and the hereafter, and brought near [to Allah]**.'" (Aal Imran 3:45)

I once read that the famous commentator Al-Baydawi reflected on this ayah. About Isa (as), he said, "His exaltation in this world is as a prophet, and in the hereafter as an intercessor."[10]

Abdullah: I was taught that there is no intercession in Islam and that we should only go to Allah (swt) to ask for forgiveness. But I know some Muslims who believe in intercession.

Isma'il: Ok. So, let's look at what the Qur'an has to say about intercession. **The Qur'an teaches us that there is someone who can intercede for us with Allah** (swt). The Qur'an also goes on to provide the qualifications for that person to be able to intercede and tells us who meets those requirements. The Qur'an says,

"Allah is the only god, living and eternal. He neither slumbers nor sleeps. Everything in the heavens and the earth is his. **Who is the one who intercedes with him except by his permission**? He knows what is in their hands and what is behind them. ..." (Al-Baqarah 2:255)

This ayah tells us that someone has to have Allah's (swt) permission to be able to intercede for others. Allah (swt) later went on to tell us that Isa (as) is the one who always does everything with His permission,

"When Allah said, '**Isa** son of Mariam, remember my blessings to you and your mother: I aided you with the Holy Spirit so you spoke to the people in the cradle and as an adult; I taught you the book, wisdom, the Tawrah and the Injil; **you create a clay bird by my permission, then you breathe into it and it becomes a bird by my permission; you heal the one born blind and the leper by my permission; you bring forth the dead by my permission**; ...'" (Al-Maidah 5:110)

The Qur'an also states that the person who intercedes has to be a witness to the Truth. It says,

"And those whom they invoke besides Allah have no power of intercession; - **only he who bears witness to the Truth**, and they know (him)." (Al-Zukhruf 43:86[2])

Isa (as) bears witness to the Truth because he is the Word of Truth. As the Qur'an states,

"**Such is Jesus (Isa)** the son of Mary [Maryam] – **the Word of Truth** about which they are in dispute." (Miriam 19:34[1])

So Abdullah, I believe that Isa al-Masih (as) has the power of intercession. Isa (as) is near to Allah (swt), Isa (as) bears witness to the Truth because he is the Truth, and Isa (as) has Allah's (swt) permission. Therefore, I can come to Allah (swt) by going through Isa.

Abdullah: Wait a minute. Earlier, you said that we had to believe in someone who is pure. I thought Allah (swt) is the only one who is pure. I heard a saying that Allah is pure and that He only accepts what is pure.[11]

Isma'il: That's true. Do you remember what the angel said to Maryam (ra) when he announced the birth of Isa al-Masih (as)?

"He said, **I** am truly a messenger from your Lord, to **give you a sinless boy**'" (Mariam 19:19)

Abdullah: Oh, I forgot that ayah (verse). That reminds me of a saying I heard that every child is touched by Satan at birth, but Isa (as) wasn't.[12]

Isma'il: I've heard that before too. But we can see clearly from the Qur'an that Isa (as) was born sinless and pure. According to the Qur'an, the angels also said,

"He [*Isa*] will speak to people in the cradle and when mature, and he is righteous." (Aal Imran 3:46)

Not only was Isa (as) born sinless and pure, but he remained sinless and pure and righteous throughout his entire life. That's because Allah (swt) breathed his Holy Spirit into Maryam (ra) the mother Isa (as), as the Qur'an said,

"We breathed of our spirit into her [*Maryam*] who guarded her chastity, and made her and her son a sign for all the universe." (Al-Anbiya 21:91)

The Qur'an tells us that Isa (as) was a spirit from Him (Allah (swt)) in (Al-Nisa 4:171). We're also told that Isa (as) was supported by the Holy Spirit throughout his entire life. In one ayah, it said,

"When Allah said, 'Isa son of Mariam, remember my blessings to you and your mother: I aided you with the Holy Spirit so you spoke to the people in the cradle and as an adult. ...'" (Al Maidah 5:110)

In several other ayat (verses), it said,

"...We brought/gave Isa son of Mariam miracles, and aided him with the Holy Spirit. ..." (Al-Baqarah 2:87, 253)

Allah's (swt) **spirit is in Isa** (as), so that's why **Isa** (as) **is holy**.

Abdullah: All right, perhaps I can agree that Isa (as) is a holy man, but how can Isa (as) do anything to help us with our faults and mistakes today?

Isma'il: There's an ayah in the Qur'an that says,

"He [***Isa***] **is knowledge of the hour**, so do not doubt it, and follow me. This is a straight path." (Al-Zukhruf 43:61)

Do you know that ayah, Abdullah?

Abdullah: Yes, I've heard that ayah before.

Isma'il: Do you believe that **Isa** (as) **is coming back again**?

Abdullah: Yes, of course, I do. And I believe that when **Isa** (as) comes back, he **will descend from heaven as a righteous judge**.[13]

Isma'il: Ok, so let me give you an illustration. Let's suppose someone commits a crime, and after that, they're arrested and brought before the judge. Now suppose **the criminal is sincerely repentant** about what he's done and **confesses his crime and begs for forgiveness and mercy**. Will the judge be merciful to him and forgive him?

Abdullah: Maybe, but I'm not sure.

Isma'il: Do you believe that **the judge has the authority to be merciful and forgive the criminal**?

Abdullah: Yes.

Isma'il: So, what if the criminal knows the judge and knows that the judge is merciful. In that case, do you think the judge will be merciful and forgive the criminal?

Abdullah: Probably.

Isma'il: Well, Abdullah, if you believe that Isa (as) is a righteous judge, you should also believe, that as a judge, Isa (as) has the authority to be merciful and forgiving. The Qur'an even tells us that **Allah** (swt) has **sent Isa** (as) **to show us His Mercy**. In the Qur'an, it says,

"He said, 'This is your Lord's saying: It is easy for me, so we will make him [**Isa**] **a sign for people, and a mercy from us.** This was **a predestined matter.**'"
(Mariam 19:21)

Since Isa (as) is Allah's (swt) mercy and Isa (as) is pure and righteous, who better is there for Allah (swt) to use in order to show us His mercy?

Abdullah: Okay, I think I'm starting to understand some interesting things you're telling me about Isa al-Masih (as). It seems that you see Isa (as) as somehow being unique. I have more questions. I don't understand how Allah's (swt) spirit could be in Isa al-Masih (as)?

Isma'il: Since Isa (as) is Allah's (swt) word and a spirit from Him. Why not?

Abdullah: But it seems strange to me that the spirit of Allah (swt) could be in a human being.

Isma'il: Why should it be strange, Abdullah? Do you know the story of Musa (as), when he was next to the mountain and saw the burning tree, and he found out that Allah (swt) was there? In that story, Allah (swt) was in the burning tree! It says,

"When he [*Musa*] came to it [*the fire*], he was **called** from the right bank of the valley, **in the tree's blessed spot**, 'Musa, **I am Allah**, Lord of the universe…'" (Al-Qasas 28:30)

In another place, it says,

"When he [*Musa*] came to it [*the fire*], he was called, '**Blessed be he who is in the fire, and he who is around it**. May Allah, the Lord of the universe, be glorified! Musa, **It is I, Allah**, mighty and wise.'" (An-Naml 27:8-9)

Abdullah: What's the meaning of this story?

Isma'il: If Allah (swt) could be in the burning tree, it means that Allah (swt) can be anywhere He wants. So, I believe that it's not impossible for Allah (swt) to live in Isa al-Masih (as) too.

Abdullah: Are you serious?

Isma'il: Abdullah, Allah (swt) can do anything. He has the power, and His power is unlimited, right?

Abdullah: Yes, but I don't think He would do that.

Isma'il: We can't limit His power. Allah (swt) has provided His own Way to show us His Compassion and Mercy. And the way that Allah (swt) has done this is by sending Isa al-Masih (as) to die and be raised alive as a mercy from Him so we could be accepted by Allah (swt).

Abdullah: Isa al-Masih (as) died and was raised alive so Allah (swt) would accept us? Hmm, that's news to me. Where did you get that idea?

Isma'il: I know that sometimes it's hard to understand Allah's (swt) Way, but that's the way Allah (swt) has done it.

Abdullah: But I've always been taught that Isa (as) didn't die. Don't you know what it says in the Qur'an?

"… 'We killed the Messiah [*al-Masih*], Isa son of Mariam, Allah's messenger,' though they did not kill him nor crucify him, but it seemed so to them. Truly those who differed about him are in doubt about him. They have no knowledge about him, but only follow what they guess. They did not slay him certainly." (Al-Nisa 4:157)

Isma'il: Yes, but look at who is the "they" in this ayah.

Abdullah: The Jews, right?

Isma'il: You're right. It was the Jews. And I agree that the Jews didn't actually kill Isa al-Masih (as). Do you know who killed Isa al-Masih (as)?

Abdullah: No. I don't know.

Isma'il: The Romans! So the Qur'an is true. **The Jews didn't kill Isa al-Masih** (as). It was **the Romans** who **killed Isa al-Masih** (as).

Abdullah: Wait a minute. What do you mean?

Isma'il: History says that the Romans crucified Isa al-Masih (as).

Abdullah: But I've been told that Allah (swt) doesn't allow any of His prophets to be killed.

Isma'il: I've heard that too, but on the contrary, the Qur'an never says that Allah (swt) doesn't allow His prophets or messengers to be killed. In fact, there are many ayat that talk about His prophets being killed. For example in one passage, it says,

"Allah has heard those [*Jews*] who said, 'Allah is poor, and we are rich.' **We will write down** their saying and **their wrongful murder of the prophets**. We will tell them, 'Taste the fire's torment.' That is for their deeds. Allah does not wrong his servants. who said, 'Allah has covenanted with us not to believe in a messenger until he brings to us an offering that fire will burn up.' Say, 'Messengers before me have come to you with miracles and with the same thing you said, **so why then did you murder them** if you are telling the truth?'" (Aal Imran 3:181-183)

Abdullah: But I've never heard a Muslim say that they believe the Romans killed Isa al-Masih (as) either.

Isma'il: That's fine. So what if I told you that Allah (swt) killed Isa al-Masih (as)?

Abdullah: No way! First, you said that the Romans killed Isa al-Masih (as), then you said that Allah (swt) killed Isa al-Masih (as). How can you have it both ways?

Isma'il: Well, Abdullah, supposed someone killed a man by stabbing him with a knife. We would say the man was killed by his murderer, and we would also say the man was killed by the knife. The Romans were like the knife in my example. I believe that Allah (swt) used them as His instrument to kill Isa al-Masih (as). And this was all planned by Allah (swt). As it says in the Qur'an,

"And they [*the Jews*] were crafty and Allah was crafty, and Allah was the craftiest. **Allah said,** '**Isa, I will** make you die and raise you up to me, and purify you from the disbelievers, ...'" (Aal Imran 3:54-55)

Do you remember the story of how Muhammad's (pbuh) men were bragging about their victory over the enemy at the battle of Badr? What does it say in the Qur'an?

"You did kill them, but Allah killed them. You did not throw when you threw, but Allah threw. He did it to test the believers well by it. Allah hears all and knows all." (Al-Anfal 8:17)

So, according to this ayah, who killed the enemy? Allah (swt) or Muhammad's (pbuh) men?

Abdullah: Both, I guess. But why would Allah (swt) kill His own messenger?

Isma'il: Allah (swt) can do anything. In the Qur'an, it says,

> "... Say: 'Who can do anything against Allah, if he wanted to destroy the Messiah [*al-Masih*], son of Mariam, his mother, and everyone on the earth?' The kingdom of the heavens, the earth, and what is between them is Allah's. He creates whatever he wills. Allah can do anything." (Al-Maidah 5:17)

Abdullah: But what would be the purpose of Allah (swt) killing Isa (as)?

Isma'il: Well, we know that the Jews wanted to kill Isa (as), and they plotted how to kill him, but Allah (swt) had His own purpose and plan. That's what it talks about when it says,

> "And they [*the Jews*] were crafty and Allah was crafty, and Allah was the craftiest." (Aal Imran 3:54)

Then it goes on to tell us what Allah's (swt) plan was in the next ayah. It says,

> "**Allah said**, '**Isa, I will** make you die and raise you up to me, and purify you from the disbelievers, and **make your followers higher than the disbelievers** until the day of resurrection. ..." (Aal Imran 3:55)

Allah (swt) had a plan: It was to provide the Way for people to be accepted by Him and to enter paradise.

Abdullah: But I'm still not sure I can believe that the Qur'an says Isa (as) died. Can you prove it?

Isma'il: We can't prove it unless we have witnesses. So first, we need to investigate it to see if we can find any witnesses.

Abdullah: Hmm, it sounds like we're watching a detective movie, and we're trying to track down the truth.

Isma'il: You're right. So, let's see if we can prove whether or not Isa al-Masih (as) died and was raised to life. Let's start with the ayah that you mentioned. It says,

> "[*The Jews said,*] 'We killed the Messiah [*al-Masih*], Isa son of Mariam, Allah's messenger,' though they did not kill him nor crucify him, but it seemed so to them. Truly those who differed about him are in doubt about him. They have no knowledge about him, but only follow what they guess. They did not slay him certainly." (Al-Nisa 4:157)

Abdullah, let me ask you something. According to this ayah, can you make a decision about whether Isa was killed or not?

Abdullah: No.

Isma'il: Why not?

Abdullah: Because **the people in this passage were in doubt about what happened**; **they didn't actually know for sure what happened**; so they just guessed about what happened. They were unsure about whether or not they had actually killed Isa (as). So, based on this ayah I wouldn't be able to make a conclusion as to whether or not Isa (as) died.

Isma'il: Ok. So imagine that we're watching a detective movie like you said, okay? And someone has been murdered. So how can the detective prove who was the killer? After he does an investigation, he'll bring the case to the court, right? But even in the court, he still can't prove what the truth is if there were no witnesses and if no one has confessed to the crime.

Abdullah: You're right. **We need witnesses**. But who are the witnesses **that can prove that Isa** (as) **died**?

Isma'il: That's a good question, Abdullah. We have two witnesses, and those two witnesses are Isa al-Masih (as) and Allah (swt)! But we need to know what their statements are.

Abdullah: You mean what Isa (as) said and what Allah (swt) said?

Isma'il: Yes! Let me show you the ayat, and the statement that was made by Isa al-Masih (as) and the statement that was made by Allah (swt). First, Isa (as) gave his statement. Isa (as) said,

"Peace be upon me the day I was born, the day I will die, and the day I will be resurrected alive!" (Maryam 19:33)

Then Allah (swt) gave this statement in the ayah that follows. Allah (swt) said,

"That is Isa the son of Mariam, **the saying of truth**, about whom **they are doubting**." (Mariam 19:34)

If we notice the second ayah, we can see that Allah (swt) confirmed Isa's (as) statement in the first ayah, that Isa (as) was born, Isa (as) died, and Isa (as) was raised to life again.

Abdullah: But Isma'il, in that ayah, Isa (as) didn't say that he had "died." He said, "die."

Isma'il: Of course, he used the word "die," not "died." Isa was still alive when he said that. How can a living person say about himself, "I died"?

Abdullah: Hmm, I guess you're right. I didn't think about that

Isma'il: So, Abdullah, what did Allah (swt) say about Isa's (as) statement? He said, "**this is the truth**."

I believe that Allah (swt) was saying something like, "Hey, listen to Me. Don't argue about it anymore. Don't dispute and doubt anymore because Isa (as) died and was raised to life from the dead!" So you see, Abdullah, it's clear from the ayat.

Abdullah: Yes, but I remember when I was at the Muslim school, we were taught that Isa (as) didn't die.

Isma'il: I was taught that too, the same as you, but if we don't believe that Isa (as) died and was raised to life, it means that we're denying what Allah (swt) said in the ayat in the Qur'an says.

Abdullah: Well, I'm confident that the Qur'an is reliable, and what it affirms is true.

Isma'il: Isa (as) spoke about his death and being raised alive, and Allah (swt) confirmed the accuracy of what he said. In the Qur'an, it says:

Allah said, "Isa, **I will** make you die and raise you up to me, and purify you from the disbelievers, and **make your followers higher than the disbelievers** until the day of resurrection. ..." (Aal Imran 3:55)

In addition, the Qur'an gives Isa's (as) own words:

"I told them only what you commanded me: 'Worship Allah, my Lord and your Lord.' I was a witness over them while I remained among them, and when you made me die, you yourself watched over them. You are witness over everything" (Al-Maidah 5:117)

We see in the ayah that Allah (swt) confirmed that Isa (as) was going to die and that Allah (swt) actually made him die.

Abdullah: Even if I agree that Isa (as) died, there are many things I still don't understand about Isa al-Masih (as). Even though you talk about Isa (as) a lot, he's still a mystery to me. Who was he, actually?

Isma'il: Abdullah, don't worry if you don't understand everything about Isa (as). What we need to do is to put our faith and trust in Allah (swt) and His word. When Isa al-Masih (as) comes back again, he's not coming back for people who just know facts about him, but for people who believe, obey and follow him. Like it says,

"But **Allah raised him [*Isa*] up** to himself. Allah is strong and wise. **Every one of the people of the book will certainly believe** in him [*Isa*] before his death, and **he [*Isa*] will be a witness over them on the day of resurrection**." (Al-Nisa 4:158-159)

Abdullah: Well, Isma'il, I still have many more questions to ask about Isa al-Masih (as), but it's time for us to go to the zoo.

❖ ଯ૭૭ଯ૭૭ଯ૭૭ଯ૭૭ଯ૭૭ଯ૭ ❖

❖ ೞೞೞೞೞೞ ❖

Chapter 4: The Zoo

We enjoyed seeing the animals at the zoo, and we took many pictures. After a while, we sat down, took some rest under a tree, and watched Abdullah's children playing in the park.

Abdullah: I truly love seeing all those animals. I especially like looking at the tigers. They have such beautiful fur. I wish I could touch them. But of course, I realize that it's impossible. They're wild animals. So I'm sure they would attack me.

Isma'il: Yes, that's true. Sadly sometimes people aren't much different than wild animals, killing each other and doing all sorts of vicious things.

Abdullah: Do you think that because Adam (as) and his wife Hawa made a mistake, that's why people aren't perfect and make mistakes now?

Isma'il: Yes. Think about it, Abdullah. Adam (as) and Hawa were disobedient, then their children were disobedient, and then all of their descendants were disobedient. We can trace what happened to them in the Qur'an. It says,

"We said, 'Adam, live with your wife in the heavenly garden and eat of it freely whatever you want, but **do not approach this tree, or you will be wicked**.'" (Al-Baqarah 2:35)

Allah (swt) gave them the freedom to do anything except approaching the one tree that Allah (swt) had forbidden. But Satan tempted them. And do you know what they did?

Abdullah: They disobeyed what Allah (swt) said.

Isma'il: You're right! The Qur'an says,

"And we had already made a covenant with Adam, but he forgot (it), and we found him lacking in steadfastness." (Taha 20:115[1])

And you know what happened after that? It goes on to say,

"and he [**Satan**] **succeeded in deceiving them**. As soon as the two had tasted (the fruit) of the tree, **their shame became obvious to them**, and they started covering themselves with leaves from the garden. Their Lord called to them, 'Did I not forbid that tree to you and tell you, 'Satan is your clear enemy?'" (Al-Aaraf 7:22[1])

Another ayah (verse) says,

"And they ate of it (*the fruit*) and **their shame was apparent to them**, and they began sewing on themselves leaves of the heavenly garden. And (thus) did **Adam disobey his Lord and went astray**." (Taha 20:121)

The ayat (verses) show us how Adam (as) and Hawa followed the advice of Satan instead of obeying Allah (swt). It also shows us the consequences of their actions. Can you imagine the shame they felt?

Abdullah: They probably felt embarrassed, hopeless, and ashamed.

Isma'il: It's no different than when we choose to disobey Allah (swt). The result is we end up feeling ashamed and full of regrets because of what we've done. The Qur'an already warns us of this. It says,

"...**the unbelievers and those who reject our signs will receive a shameful punishment**." (Al-Hajj 22:57[1])

Would you want to live your life full of shame and regret and experience the same thing forever in the hereafter?

Abdullah: Of course not! So, what do think Allah's reaction was to what Adam (as) and Hawa did?

Isma'il: Undoubtedly, Allah (swt) was displeased with their choice. He didn't want them to follow Satan. But the Qur'an tells us,

"Then Satan whispered to him, saying, 'Adam, shall I show you the tree of immortality and a kingdom that will never decay?'" (Taha 20:120[1])

Abdullah: It seems that Satan promised them immortality and more. It's no wonder they listened to Satan.

Isma'il: Yes, but Allah (swt) had already told them that Satan was their enemy. In the Qur'an, Allah (swt) said,

"So we said, 'O Adam, this [*Satan*] is an enemy to you and to your wife. Do not let him drive you out of the garden and make you suffer.'" (Taha 20:117[1])

Abdullah: So Adam (as) and Hawa ended up in a bad situation, didn't they?

Isma'il: Not only Adam (as) and Hawa, but their children too. The Qur'an says,

"Tell them the truth about the story of Adam's two sons -- how each of them offered a sacrifice, one being accepted and the other being rejected. One said, 'I will kill you!' The other replied, '**God [*Allah*] only accepts the sacrifice of those who are mindful of him**.'" (Al-Maidah 5:27[1])

And you can also see it later in the ayat that followed,

"His selfishness caused him to murder his brother. He killed him and **became doomed**." (Al-Maidah 5:30[1])

But Qabil (Cain) wasn't the only evildoer. After that, the Qur'an tells us that **everyone is disobedient**. It says,

"Who granted you all you asked Him. Were you to count the bounties of God [*Allah*], you could not take stock of them. **Man is indeed wicked and most ungrateful**."
(Ibrahim 14:34[3])

Another ayah says,

"We offered a trust for safekeeping to the heavens, the earth, and the mountains, and they refused to bear it, and feared it. **Mankind** took it, and they **were wicked and foolish**." (Al-Ahzab 33:72)

So you see, Abdullah, **all people are wicked and foolish unbelievers**, not just a few.

Abdullah: Well, we're only human. We all make mistakes sometimes.

Isma'il: It's not just a little mistake, Abdullah. We are all just as disobedient as Adam (as) and Hawa in that we continually choose to disobey Allah (swt) and do the things Allah (swt) has forbidden.

Abdullah: Okay, maybe we all have the desire to disobey Allah (swt) once in a while, but don't you think Allah (swt) still loved Adam (as) and Hawa? After all, He forgave them, right?

Isma'il: Yes, He loved them, and He promised to forgive them, but only if they followed His guidance.

Abdullah: His guidance? What guidance?

Isma'il: In the Qur'an it says,

"Then his Lord chose him [*Adam*], accepted his repentance, and guided him." (Taha 20:122)

Do you know what that **guidance** is, Abdullah?

Abdullah: I'm not sure.

Isma'il: Earlier in the Qur'an it tells us,

"We revealed the Tawrah, in which is guidance and light. The prophets who submitted, the rabbis, and the priests judge the Jews according to the portion of Allah's book with which they have been entrusted. They were witnesses of it. So do not fear people, but fear me, and do not sell my verses for a small price. Whoever does not judge by what Allah has revealed are disbelievers. ... **We made Isa** son of Mariam **follow in their footsteps, confirming the Tawrah** in his possession, **and**

we gave him the Injil, in which is guidance and light, confirming the Tawrah in his possession, **as guidance and an admonition to the godly**." (Al-Maidah 5:44 and 46)

Abdullah: What's your point, Isma'il?

Isma'il: Well, after Adam (as) and Hawa were disobedient, Allah (swt) accepted their repentance, covered their shame, and exhorted them to follow His Guidance. The Qur'an makes it clear that Allah (swt) accepted their repentance. We're told that several times. In one place, it says,

"Adam received words from his Lord, who accepted his repentance. He is the merciful accepter of repentance." (Al-Baqarah 2:37)

We're also told how Allah (swt) provided the Way to cover their shame. The Qur'an says,

"O ye Children of Adam! We have bestowed raiment upon you to cover your shame, as well as to be an adornment to you. But the raiment of righteousness, - that is the best. Such are among the Signs of Allah, that they may receive admonition!" (Al-Aaraf 7:26[2])

Allah (swt) also gave a promise to Adam (as) and Hawa, that whoever would follow His Guidance wouldn't fear or have reason to grieve. According to the Qur'an, Allah (swt) declared,

"We said, 'All of you go down from it (the garden). **When my guidance comes to you, whoever follows my guidance will not have fear** or grieve.'" (Al-Baqarah 2:38)

Like we just saw, the Qur'an goes on to say that the Tawrah and Injil that were given later are guidance and light. So it explains that we have to follow Allah's (swt) Guidance and Light, which is in the Tawrah and Injil. Then Allah (swt) will keep us from fear.

Abdullah: Ah, I think I'm beginning to understand why Allah (swt) sent Isa (as). I think Allah (swt) sent Isa (as) with the Injil to bring us the light of Allah (swt).

Isma'il: Yes, Abdullah, Allah (swt) sent Isa (as) to confirm the Truth and to bring us Allah's (swt) Guidance and Light. But the truth is, we're all disobedient, just as Adam (as) and Hawa were disobedient, and we're afraid of the consequences of our disobedience and what we'll face in the future. Allah (swt) has given us His Compassion and Mercy, so we don't have to face the torment of Hell. Allah (swt) has sent Isa al-Masih (as) to show us His Mercy. So we don't have to be afraid anymore about what will happen to us after we die.

Abdullah: But Isma'il, I still don't understand why Allah (swt) would send Isa (as) to show us His mercy. What is the connection between Isa al-Masih (as) and the Mercy of Allah (swt)?

Isma'il: Abdullah, Allah (swt) sent Isa al-Masih (as) as a Mercy for all people to save us from the torment of hell. As it says in the Qur'an,

"He said, "This is your Lord's saying: It is easy for me, so we will make him [*Isa*] **a sign for people, and a mercy from us**. This was **a predestined matter.**" (Mariam 19:21)

Abdullah: Hmm, I don't fully understand.

Isma'il: It's okay, let me try to explain. When I think about Allah (swt), there are things that I don't fully understand either. But the Qur'an doesn't teach us to rely on our own understanding only. It also teaches us to trust in Allah (swt), then Allah (swt) will give us more understanding. Abdullah, have you ever noticed when you read the Qur'an how many passages start with the word "**Believers**..."? It doesn't say, "You who understand, ..."

Abdullah: Yes, I know. I've recited the ayat (verses), but I'm a believer, not an unbeliever. So what are you trying to say?

Isma'il: What I'm trying to say is this, that most people are afraid of dying, and do you know why? It's because they don't truly know and **believe** what Allah (swt) has revealed. And since they don't **believe**, they don't have any assurance because they don't know what will happen after they die. So they're afraid of what will happen on the judgment day.

Abdullah: I can understand that. I'm afraid of dying and of the Day of Judgment too. So, how do you know what will happen to you on the Day of Judgment?

Isma'il: I wouldn't know what would happen to me after I die unless I had someone to tell me. But I already know someone who knows what will happen to me on the judgment day.

Abdullah: What do you mean?

Isma'il: Let me give you an example. Let's say you're planning to go to a city in another country that you've never been to before. I don't think you would go there without knowing someone who lives there, right?

Abdullah: Yes, that's probably true.

Isma'il: And why?

Abdullah: I guess I could get lost there since I don't know the streets or how to get around anywhere. But, on the other hand, I could buy a map and find the directions from the map.

Isma'il: Yes, but wouldn't you agree that the information on the map probably came from someone who's been there before?

Abdullah: Yes, you're probably right.

Isma'il: So you see, you need someone who can tell you where things are and how to find your way around in that city?

Abdullah: Okay.

Isma'il: So if you know someone in the place where you're going, or know someone who has been there before, they can tell you where you want to go and how to get there, then you don't need to worry about being lost.

Abdullah: Yes, but sometimes it might be more exciting and adventurous, not knowing exactly where you're going. Who knows the interesting stories you might have to tell afterward.

Isma'il: Well, that might be true sometimes when you're on a trip. But what we're actually getting at is what will happen after you die. Do you really want to take a chance and end up in the wrong place?

Abdullah: Okay, that's a good point, Isma'il.

Isma'il: Besides that, as I told you, most people are afraid of dying and fearful of the judgment day because they don't know what will happen after they die, and they're afraid of being judged.

Abdullah: Yes, most of my friends say that they're afraid of death and judgment. But they think that no one can know what will happen after they die.

Isma'il: That sounds like the sort of people I was referring to in my story. They're going to a city in another country, but they don't have a clue about how to get there or about what would happen if they ever got there. We can be certain that they'll end up being lost.

Abdullah: What about you, Isma'il? Are you afraid of what will happen after you die?

Isma'il: I'm not afraid of what will happen to me when I die, and I'm not fearful of what will happen to me on the Day of Judgment or in the Hereafter.

Abdullah: How can you say that? It sounds like you're boasting. Besides that, I think no one can know what will happen after they die. Only Allah (swt) knows that.

Isma'il: I'm not boasting, Abdullah. I have assurance and peace about what will happen to me after I die. It's not based on something that I've dreamed up in my own mind. It's because of Isa al-Masih (as). The Qur'an says,

"When the angels said, 'Mariam, Allah gives you good news of a word from him, whose name will be the Messiah, **Isa** son of Mariam, **highly exalted in this world and the hereafter, and brought near [to Allah].**'" (Aal Imran 3:45)

Abdullah: So how can Isa (as) help you?

Isma'il: It's just like in the story I told you about, of a person going to a foreign city. If they went to a foreign city that they'd never been to before, they'd be lost there if they didn't know anyone there. But unlike that person, I already know someone who is in the Hereafter. Alhamdulillah, I know **Isa al-Masih** (as) **who is near stationed to Allah** (swt). **He is highly exalted in this world and the Hereafter**. So when I die, I will not be lost.

Abdullah: But what about the day of judgment? Aren't you afraid of that?

Isma'il: Why should I be? I know that Isa al-Masih (as) was sent by Allah (swt) and that Isa (as) knows what will happen on the Day of Judgment. As it says in the Qur'an,

> **"He [*Isa*] is knowledge of the hour**, so do not doubt it, and follow me. This is a straight path." (Al-Zukhruf 43:61)

It also says,

> "Every one of the people of the book will certainly believe in him [*Isa*] before his death, and he [*Isa*] will be a witness over them on the day of resurrection." (Al-Nisa 4:159)

Since I already believe, obey, and follow Isa al-Masih (as) as a Mercy from Allah (swt), I don't have to worry about the judgment day because Isa (as) will be my witness.

Abdullah: I believe that Isa al-Masih (as) will come back to this world for a second time.

Isma'il: Yes, I agree. Many Muslims believe that too. Imagine when Isa al-Masih (as) comes back to this world. Millions of people will see him. I believe that many people will pretend to be eager to meet him, but Isa (as) will know which people are his true followers.

Abdullah: What do you mean, he will recognize the people who have truly followed him? You mean Christians, right?

Isma'il: What I mean is anyone who believes, obeys, and follows Isa (as). It doesn't matter what their religion is. Isa (as) didn't tell people to become Christians. In the Qur'an,

> "When **Isa** brought miracles, he **said**, 'I have come to you with wisdom, and to clarify to you your differences, so **fear Allah and obey me**. Allah is my Lord and your Lord, so worship him. **This is a straight path**.'" (Al-Zukhruf 43:63-64)

Also, when Allah (swt) said He would exalt the followers of Isa (as), He didn't use the term Christians. The Qur'an says,

> **"Allah said, 'Isa, I will** make you die and raise you up to me, and purify you from the disbelievers, and **make your followers higher than the disbelievers** until the day of resurrection. ...'" (Aal Imran 3:55)

Abdullah: But how can you say from any religion? I thought only Christians were followers of Isa al-Masih (as).

Isma'il: Some people were born into a Christian family, so they're called Christians because their family is Christian, but it doesn't mean that they actually believe, obey or follow Isa al-Masih (as). It won't help them any on the day of judgment to be called Christians if they haven't believed, obeyed, and followed Isa (as) and if they don't know Isa (as) as a predestined Mercy from Allah (swt).

Abdullah: So you're saying that not all Christians are believers, right? Then how can I tell the difference between a Christian who is a true believer and follower of Isa (as) and one who isn't?

Isma'il: A true follower of Isa (as) believes that **it's by the Compassion and Mercy of Allah** (swt) **that they are made righteous and have forgiveness, and not by their good works or effort alone**. Isn't this what the Qur'an teaches? As Allah says in the Qur'an,

> "... If **Allah's grace and mercy** had not been on you, none of you would ever be pure, but **Allah purifies** those he wills. Allah hears all and knows all." (An-Nur 24:21)

We're also given an example of this in the story of the prophet Yunus (as). The Qur'an says,

> "If blessings from his Lord had not come to him [*Yunus*], he would have been left disgraced in a deserted place. But his Lord chose him and made him righteous." (Al-Qalam 68:49-50)

A true follower of Isa (as) believes that **Allah** (swt) **has rescued them from the torment of hell.** Just as Allah (swt) rescued Ibrahim's (as) son **with a great sacrifice** in Al-Saffat 37:107, so they believe that Allah (swt) has rescued them from punishment **with a great sacrifice** through **the death of Isa al-Masih** (as).

A true follower of Isa (as) also believes that Allah (swt) has made them alive spiritually through Isa al-Masih (as). I remember reading somewhere that Isa al-Masih (as) said, "Whoever has not been born twice will not enter the Kingdom of Heaven."[14]

Abdullah: How do you know all that?

Isma'il: Well, even though we live in a Muslim neighborhood and most of our friends are Muslims, some of my coworkers at work are from other religions. I have some Buddhist, Christian, and Hindu coworkers. My Christian coworkers are always friendly and respectful to me even though they know I'm a Muslim. Sometimes when we talk, we don't just talk about our jobs, but we also talk about business, politics, and even talk about spiritual things. Anyway, there's nothing wrong with asking them questions about what they believe. In the Qur'an, Allah (swt) told the prophet Muhammad (pbuh) to ask the People of the Book if he had questions about what Allah (swt) showed him. It says,

> "So **when you are in doubt about what we have revealed to you, ask those who are reading the book that was before you**. Truth has come to you from your Lord, so **do not be a doubter**." (Yunus 10:94)

Abdullah: Everyone knows that Christians believe in three gods: Allah (swt), Isa (as), and Maryam (ra). So how could you dare to ask Christians about anything when they worship three gods?

Isma'il: I'm not surprised that you say that, Abdullah. I used to think that too. So when I met with my Christian coworkers, I asked them about it. They said that the true followers of Isa believe in one God – Allah (swt), his word, and his spirit. They also told me that they don't believe that Maryam (ra) is a god or goddess.

Abdullah: What do you mean? That still sounds like two gods in addition to Allah (swt).

Isma'il: Well, they said that the true followers of Isa believe in one God, as it says in the Qur'an,

"Do not argue with the people of the book but [speak] in a fair manner, except with the wicked among them. Say, "We believe in what was revealed to us and what was revealed to you. **Our god and your god is one**, and we submit to him." (Al-Ankabut 29:46)

My Christian coworkers told me that in Muhammad's (pbuh) time, there was a zanadiqa (heresy) where some religious groups believed in three gods, or that believed that Maryam (ra) was a goddess. I'm sure from this ayah that the followers of Isa al-Masih (as) only believe in one God the same as we as Muslims believe in Allah (swt).

Abdullah: So, what do they mean when they say they believe in Allah (swt), his word, and his spirit?

Isma'il: That's a good question. What do we mean when we say "Bismillah al-Rahman al-Rahim:" in the name of Allah (swt), the most Gracious, the Merciful? Are we saying that Allah (swt), al-Rahman, and al-Rahim are three separate gods?

Abdullah: No. Allah (swt) is One!

Isma'il: Okay. So what if we're reciting the Ninety-nine Beautiful Names? Are we worshipping many gods or one?

Abdullah: One!

Isma'il: You're right, Abdullah. So we have to learn about the true beliefs of the followers of Isa al-Masih first before we make a judgment about them. Otherwise, we might reach the wrong conclusion about what they believe.

Abdullah: But I've heard that there are many ayat in the Qur'an that say Christians are bad and Christians are evil.

Isma'il: The ayat are only saying that some of the People of the Book are like that. It doesn't mean that all of them are like that. The Qur'an says,

"They are not all alike. Among the people of the book are upright people, reading God's [*Allah's*] verses all night as they bow down." (Aal Imran 3:113[1])

There's also another ayah that says,

"Among the people of the book are those who believe in God [*Allah*] and what was revealed to you and what was revealed to them. They stand in awe of God [*Allah*]; they do not barter God's [*Allah's*] messages for trivial gain. They have their reward from their Lord: God [*Allah*] is quick in settling accounts." (Aal Imran 3:199[1])

Abdullah: So, when you're discussing religious things with your Christian coworkers, what happens if you don't agree with them about their beliefs or practices? Do you get angry or upset with them?

Isma'il: No, Abdullah. That would be wrong. The Qur'an says that we have to be friendly with them, as it says in the ayah I referred to before,

"Do not argue with the people of the book but [speak] in a fair manner, …" (Al-Ankabut 29:46)

It means that if we discuss things with the People of the Book, it should be in the friendliest possible manner. So I don't have a problem with discussing religious or spiritual things with my coworkers.

Abdullah: Hmm. So did your Christian coworkers ever talk to you about Isa al-Masih (as)?

Isma'il: Yes, sometimes. Anyway, I like hanging out with my coworkers, because when we get together for our lunch break or when we go out together after work, we talk about many things, not just work.

Abdullah: So what sorts of things do you usually talk about with them?

Isma'il: Everyday life, family, and work. Recently one of my coworkers had some problems that he wanted to talk about, and he was looking for advice. I tried to encourage him to have faith in the Compassion and Mercy of Allah (swt) and not to doubt. I advised him to read the Holy Books so that he could find Guidance and Light from Allah (swt).

Abdullah: Do your coworkers accept your advice?

Isma'il: Yes, especially those who believe and follow Isa al-Masih (as). Allah (swt) has promised them victory over their problems in contrast to the unbelievers who have no one to turn to for help and have no assurance of what will happen to them now or in the hereafter. As it says in the Qur'an,

"Allah said, 'Isa, **I will** make you die and raise you up to me, and purify you from the disbelievers, and **make your followers higher than the disbelievers** until the day of resurrection. Then you will return to me and I will judge between you in matters about which you differ.'" (Aal Imran 3:55)

But about the unbelievers, Allah (swt) said,

"… **I will severely punish the unbelievers** both in this world and the hereafter, and **they will have no one to help them**.'" (Aal Imran 3:56[1])

Abdullah: You know what, Isma'il? It looks like it's going to rain soon, so maybe we should go home before we get wet.

Isma'il: You're right, Abdullah. But before we go, I want to let you know that I'll be having a small party at my house next weekend. I'd like to invite you to come if you have time.

Abdullah: What's the party for?

Isma'il: It's for my brother. We want to celebrate because Allah (swt) helped him to get a new
job.

Abdullah: That's great! Alhamdulillah! So, I'll see you then. Assalamu'alaikum.

Isma'il: Wa'alaikum salam.

❖ ∞෬∞෬∞෬∞෬∞෬∞෬ ❖

✧❀❀❀❀❀❀❀❀❀❀✧

Chapter 5: A Celebration

Over the weekend, Abdullah came to my house for a celebration with my brother and some other friends because my brother got a new job. We had the party outside in the garden behind the house. After everyone had left, Abdullah and I went into the sitting room for some additional conversation.

Isma'il: Alhamdulillah, my brother got a new job. He had only been unemployed for a short time. We prayed, and then suddenly, he got a new job. And amazingly the new job is even better than the one he used to have. Allah (swt) is good. He's so Compassionate and Merciful to us.

Abdullah: You're always talking about the Mercy of Allah (swt). What do you mean when you talk about the Mercy of Allah (swt)?

Isma'il: **The Mercy of Allah** (swt) **is something free from Allah** (swt). **There's nothing we can do to earn it and no way that we could ever pay Him back**. Can I give you an example?

Abdullah: Okay, sure.

Isma'il: As a teacher, I encounter students cheating on papers and exams. At the beginning of a course, I explain that the consequences for cheating will be receiving zero credit for the paper or exam, and they will not be allowed to redo it. Now suppose I caught a student cheating on an exam, and I gave him zero credit for the exam. Did I have mercy on the student?

Abdullah: No, you gave the student what he deserved.

Isma'il: What if I knew that a student cheated and I confronted the student with the evidence, and I tell the student that I will give him another exam, and if he passes the exam, he will receive a minimum passing grade for it. Do you think I showed mercy then?

Abdullah: Yes, it would mean that you showed mercy. The student should have received zero credit, but you gave him another chance.

Isma'il: Well, Abdullah, **Allah** (swt) **has freely given us Isa al-Masih** (as) **as His predestined Mercy**. We're told this in the Qur'an when it says,

"He said, 'This is your Lord's saying: It is easy for me, so we will make him [**Isa**] **a sign for people, and a mercy from us.** This was **a predestined matter.**'" (Mariam 19:21)

Another ayah (verse) tells us why we need Allah's (swt) mercy. It says,

"… If **Allah's grace and mercy** had not been on you, none of you would ever be pure, …" (Al-Nur 24:21)

Abdullah: I know that **Allah is Compassionate and Merciful**. But how can I be sure that I will receive His Mercy?

Isma'il: **By putting your faith and trust in Isa al-Masih** (as) **as the predestined Mercy of Allah** (swt) so that Allah (swt) will purify you.

Abdullah: What do I need to do to put my faith and trust in the predestined Mercy of Allah (swt)?

Isma'il: **Allah** (swt) **tells us to repent and believe**. Just as it says in the Qur'an,

"Your Lord is forgiving and merciful toward those who do bad deeds and later repent and believe." (Al-Aaraf 7:153)

Repentance brings about a change of heart and mind so that we will think differently.

Abdullah: What do you mean, change my heart and mind and think differently?

Isma'il: I mean that it's not enough to believe that Allah (swt) will accept us just because of our good works. We **must also believe that it is by the Compassion and Mercy of Allah** (swt) **in Isa al-Masih** (as) **that we can be accepted by Allah** (swt). **Then we can know the Compassion, Mercy, Forgiveness, and Peace that comes from Allah** (swt)!

Abdullah: I can certainly see that Allah (swt) has shown His Compassion and Mercy to your brother by helping him get a new job so quickly. Anyway, I'm glad your brother got a good job. I'm very happy for him.

Isma'il: And how is your job, Abdullah?

Abdullah: Alhamdulillah. I've got a fantastic job and a good salary. Everything's going well at my work, and I don't have any financial problems.

Isma'il: That's great, Abdullah.

Abdullah: But even though everything's going well at home and work, sometimes I don't feel satisfied. I mean, the money and all the things I have don't truly make me happy.

Isma'il: You mean you're not content even with all of that?

Abdullah: That's right. How can you have satisfaction, Isma'il? You're only a teacher. You said that your teaching position doesn't pay a high salary. But when I see your smiling face, I can tell that you're always full of happiness and peace.

Isma'il: Abdullah, even though my salary isn't much, I still thank Allah (swt) for everything He has given to me. Besides that, nothing in this world lasts forever anyway. But I have peace because **I believe in Isa** (as), who **has peace**. In the Qur'an, Isa (as) said,

"**Peace** be upon me the day I was born, the day I will die, and the day I will be resurrected alive!" (Mariam 19:33)

As I told you before, no one can say 'peace be upon me' unless they have the authority to pronounce peace. I have peace because **Isa** (as), who **has peace**, **has given me peace**.

Abdullah: I don't have peace. I feel dead inside.

Isma'il: Do you remember the story about Isa (as) and the bird? I think we talked about this story before. It's the story about how Isa (as) breathed into a clay bird and made it become a **live** bird. It says,

"When Allah said, 'Isa son of Mariam, remember my blessings to you and your mother: I aided you with the Holy Spirit so you spoke to the people in the cradle and as an adult. I taught you the book, wisdom, the Tawrah and the Injil. You create a clay bird by my permission, then you breathe into it and it becomes a bird by my permission. You heal the one born blind and the leper by my permission. **You bring forth the dead** by my permission. I kept the people of Israel from you when you brought them miracles.' But the disbelievers among them said: 'This is just magic.'" (Al-Maidah 5:110)

The Qur'an also says that Allah (swt) would send Isa (as),

"[And Isa was] a messenger to the people of Israel, 'I have brought you a sign from your Lord: I create a bird for you from clay and breathe into it and it will be a [living] bird by Allah's permission. **I heal the man born blind and the leper and give life to the dead by Allah's permission**. I tell you what you eat and what you store in your houses. **That is** truly **a sign for you, if you believe**.'" (Aal Imran 3:49)

Abdullah: Yes, I remember we talked about that story before. It's an amazing story!!

Isma'il: Look at what Isa (as) can do. He can make a bird out of clay and then has the power to make the clay bird become a live bird. Not only that, but Isa (as) even has the power to raise dead people to life. **Allah** (swt) **gave authority to Isa to give life** to the clay bird and raise dead people to life again. It means that Isa (as) has the power not only to give physical life but to give spiritual life also. That's why **I put my trust in Isa** (as) **as the life-giver**. **He has given me spiritual life**.

Abdullah: You know, Isma'il, I've been thinking about what you told me about Isa al-Masih (as), but I still have many questions. Can you explain more to me about what we have to believe and what we have to do to obey and follow Isa al-Masih (as)?

Isma'il: If you have time right now, we can look at some ayat (verses) in the Qur'an and see what they say. I think we've discussed many of the passages before.

Abdullah: Sure, I have time.

Isma'il: I have a Qur'an here. You can read the ayat with me, and then I'll give you some comments on the ayat.

1. Taha 20:121 says,
"And they ate of it and their shame was apparent to them, and they began sewing on themselves leaves of the heavenly garden. Adam disobeyed his Lord and went astray."

This ayah shows us how our ancestors Adam (as) **and Hawa errored by disobeying Allah** (swt).

2. Al-Ahzab 33:72 says,
"We offered a trust for safekeeping to the heavens and the earth, and the mountains, and they refused to bear it, and feared it. **Mankind** took it, and **they were wicked and foolish**."

This ayah shows us that since then, **everyone is erring. All people are wayward and have gone astray, not just a few people. We have all proven ourselves to be irresponsible and unworthy of Allah's** (swt) **trust.**

3. Taha 20:74 says,
"He who comes to his Lord as a wrongdoer will go to hell, where he will neither die nor live."

This ayah shows us that Allah (swt) **is Holy and Pure. We can't come into His presence with our faults. Otherwise, Allah** (swt) **will send us to Hell for eternity.**

4. Al-Maidah 5:95[1] says,
"Believers, do not hunt while you are in the state for sanctity. Whoever kills an animal intentionally must make amends by offering an equivalent domestic animal comparable to what was killed as defined by two just men – an offering to be delivered to the Ka'bah. Or, he may atone for his sin by feeding the needy, or by fasting an equivalent number of days, so that he may understand the seriousness of what he has done. God [*Allah*] forgives what is past, but if anyone does it again, God [*Allah*] will punish him severely. God [*Allah*] is mighty, and capable of exacting the penalty."

This ayah shows us that if we disobey Allah's commands, no matter how big or small, we have to pay for it. And sin should be paid for in an amount equivalent to what we have sinned. We sin over and over, so if we keep on committing sin, in the end, how great will be the amount we owe?

5. Al-Maidah 5:27[1] says,

"Tell them the truth about the story of Adam's two sons -- how each of them offered a sacrifice, one being accepted and the other being rejected. One said, 'I will kill you!' The other replied, '**God [*Allah*] only accepts the sacrifice of those who are mindful of him**.'"

And Al-Hajj 22:37[2] says,

"**It is not their meat nor their blood that reaches Allah**: it is your piety that reaches Him: ..."

The ayat show us how people tried to offer animals as a sacrifice believing that the meat and blood would be successful in appeasing Allah (swt)**, but the Qur'an says they don't avail with Allah** (swt)**. People started offering sacrifices to Allah** (swt)**, but Allah** (swt) **only accepts the sacrifice from a righteous person. But how can anyone be righteous since everyone has disobeyed Allah?**

6. Al-Nur 24:21 says,

"... If **Allah's grace and mercy** had not been on you, none of you would ever be pure, but **Allah purifies** those he wills. Allah hears all and knows all."

Al-Qalam 68:49-50 says,

"If blessings from his Lord had not come to him [*Yunus*], he would have been left disgraced in a deserted place. But his Lord chose him and made him righteous."

These passages show us that we cannot make ourselves righteous. Allah (swt) **is the source of righteousness, and He makes people righteous, so we cannot earn it by doing good deeds or offering sacrifices.**

7. Al-Maidah 5:33[1] says,

"Those who war against God [*Allah*] and his messenger and who strive to spread corruption on earth should **be punished by death, crucifixion, the amputation of their hands and their feet**, or **should be entirely banished** from (the face of) the earth. **Such is their disgrace in this world. In the Hereafter, a terrible punishment awaits them--**"

It means that the punishment for **dishonorable and reprobate people** is that they **have to be killed, crucified**, have their **hands and feet mutilated**, or be expelled from the land. **They will be humiliated in this world**, and even worse than that, they will **have terrible punishment in the hereafter**.

So, Abdullah, after you looked at all of these statements, do you think we can escape from punishment and the torment of hell?

Abdullah: After hearing about all of the punishments that Allah (swt) has decreed for those who disobey Allah (swt) and go astray, I think we can't escape from punishment and the torment of hell.

Isma'il: Why?

Abdullah: Because when I think about it, I realize no one is perfect. We all make mistakes sometimes, and nobody is completely pure either.

Isma'il: So, we deserve the punishment, right?

Abdullah: Yes, I suppose so. But why are you telling me this?

Isma'il: The reason I'm telling you this is because I wanted you to **think about how serious and horrible the consequences of disobeying Allah** (swt) **truly are**!!! Can you imagine the kinds of punishment we will get because of our misdeeds?

Abdullah: It's too frightening, so I don't want to think about it.

Isma'il: So Abdullah, how about if you read the ayah to me from your Qur'an?

Abdullah: I'd rather not.

Isma'il: So, I take it that you don't want to receive those punishments, do you?

Abdullah: Of course not!

Isma'il: Well, neither do I. I don't believe anybody truly wants to receive those kinds of horrible punishments.

Abdullah: I truly hope that doesn't happen to me.

Isma'il: Sorry, Abdullah, but it will happen to all who have errored and gone astray and disobeyed Allah (swt).

Abdullah: But **Allah** (swt) **is forgiving**.

Isma'il: Yes, **but Allah** (swt) **is just too. Everyone who has disobeyed Allah** (swt) **deserves to be punished**.

Abdullah: But **Allah** (swt) is **Compassionate** and **Merciful**.

Isma'il: Yes, you're absolutely right, Abdullah. That's why **Allah** (swt) **has provided the Way for us to be saved from the punishments in Hell**.

Abdullah: How?

Isma'il: Let's look at Al-Maidah 5:33 again. I'll read it from your Qur'an this time.

"Those who war against God [Allah] and his messenger and who strive to spread corruption on earth should be **punished by death, crucifixion, the amputation of their hands and their feet**, or should be entirely banished from (the face of) the earth. **Such is their disgrace in this world. In the Hereafter, a terrible punishment awaits them**--" (Al-Maidah 5:33[1])

Please consider all of the things that we deserve: **to be killed, to be crucified, to have hands and feet severed, to be expelled from the land, to be humiliated in this world, and have terrible punishment in the Hereafter**.

After we've thought about all the things that we deserve because of all our mistakes, think about this: **What if Allah** (swt) **came to you and said**,

"Abdullah, **I am just, I have to punish you because of all your mistakes, but** on the other hand, **I love** you so much. Because **I am Compassionate and Merciful, I don't want you** to have **to endure the terrible punishment. I have provided the Way to save you from the punishment. Take My Way as a Mercy from Me for free. Here is My Mercy.** I have **SOMEONE** who is **willing to take your punishment. He was born by My Holy Spirit. He is My Word. He was born as Our Mercy. He is Sinless and Pure. He has been killed for you. He has been crucified for you. His hands and feet were wounded for your punishment. I raised him from the dead, so you could be victorious over death and have life in Paradise too. He will help you in this world and the Hereafter** because **I have made Him highly exalted in this world and the Hereafter.** And if you **accept him to replace your punishment, then you are free from the judgment!**"

Now Abdullah, Allah (swt) is fair, isn't He?

Abdullah: Yes.

Isma'il: So, if Allah (swt) offered to provide you with **SOMEONE** like that, would you accept His offer?

Abdullah: Of course I'd accept His offer. It would be foolish of me to reject **SOMEONE** who has offered to take my place and be punished instead of me... if Allah (swt) gave me **SOMEONE** who was willing to be punished for me. I would bow before Allah (swt) and thank Allah (swt) for His Compassion and Mercy to give me **SOMEONE** to take the punishment for my mistakes.

Isma'il: It's not just a story, Abdullah. Allah (swt) truly loves us!!! He sent Isa al-Masih (as) to take our punishment. If we believe in Isa (as) as the great sacrifice that Allah (swt) has provided to ransom us, then we will not be condemned to punishment and torment in Hell. **Isa** (as) **was killed, he was crucified, his hands and his feet were wounded**. He did all of that to take the punishment that we deserved.

In Aal Imran 3:55, it says that **Allah** (swt) caused Isa al-Masih (as) to die and raised him to life again and then took Isa (as) to be with Himself. As a result, Allah (swt) promised to exalt Isa's (as) followers far above unbelievers.

"Allah said, 'Isa, I will make you die and raise you to me, and purify you from the disbelievers, and **make your followers higher than the disbelievers** until the day of resurrection. ..." (Aal Imran 3:55)

So, Abdullah, if we believe in Isa al-Masih (as) and follow him, we will be exalted and live in Paradise.

Abdullah: I've always thought that by trying to be a good person and by doing good works, Allah (swt) would accept me. And I've always hoped that Allah (swt) would let me into Paradise. But now you've told me **it is only by the Compassion and Mercy of Allah** (swt) **by obeying and following Isa al-Masih** (as) **that Allah** (swt) **can accept me**. Exactly how can we receive Allah's (swt) Compassion and Mercy?

Isma'il: Do you want to call on Isa al-Masih (as) now?

Abdullah: I wouldn't know what the proper dua (prayer of supplication) would be.

Isma'il: How about if I pray for us instead?

Abdullah: Sure. Thank you, Isma'il.

Isma'il: Bismillah. Allahumma, I want to thank You so much Allah (swt) for revealing the Qur'an and for sending the prophet Muhammad (pbuh), who came as a warner, to warn me about how terrible the punishment would be for a disobedient person like me. I would also like to thank You, Allah (swt), for showing me Your Compassion and Your Mercy by sending Isa al-Masih (as) to take the shameful punishment I deserved in place of me. Thank you, Allah (swt), for giving us Isa (as), who is exalted in this world and the next, and an intercessor on my behalf. And thank You, Allah (swt), for resurrecting Isa (as) from the dead and raising him to heaven, so I too could be raised to life in paradise in the Hereafter. Amen.

Since then, Abdullah and I have continued meeting together for spiritual discussions and prayers.

❖⊰⊱⊰⊱⊰⊱⊰⊱⊰⊱❖

Epilogue:

"Those who war against God [Allah] and his messenger and who strive to spread corruption on earth should be **punished by death, crucifixion, the amputation of their hands and their feet**, or should be entirely banished from (the face of) the earth. **Such is their disgrace in this world. In the Hereafter, a terrible punishment awaits them**--"
(Al-Maidah 5:33[1])

"Except for those who repent before you overpower them. You must bear in mind that God [*Allah*] is forgiving and Merciful-to-all."
(Al-Maidah 5:34[1])

Alhamdulillah! We thank Allah (swt) that we can have forgiveness, freedom from shame, and peace from Allah (swt) while we are still alive in this world. How terrible it would be for us if we died before we knew the Compassion and Mercy of Allah (swt) that He gave us through Isa al-Masih (as).

Alhamdulilah, We thank Allah (swt) for showing us that **it is only by the Compassion and Mercy of Allah** (swt) **in Isa al-Masih** (as) **that we can have forgiveness, peace, and eternal life in paradise**.

Alhamdulillah, we thank Allah (swt) that He has enlightened our hearts to know the Straight Way of His Compassion and Mercy through Isa al-Masih (as) who was willing to be killed and crucified and let his hands and feet be wounded and hurt to take the punishment that should have been ours in this world and the Hereafter.

"I pray that you will have **peace** as a result of reading this book." – *Isma'il*

May Allah (swt) enlighten your heart
to know
His Compassion and His Mercy.
Amen.

Assalamua'laikum wa rohmatullahi wabarakatuh

❖ ✿ꋬꇸ✿ꋬꇸ✿ꋬꇸ✿ꋬꇸ✿ꋬꇸ✿ꋬ ❖

Notes:

[Unless otherwise identified, the verses from the Qur'an that were used in this story are from the Reference Qur'an translation, used by permission and available at referencequran.com.]

1– *The Qur'an - with References to the Bible: A Contemporary Understanding*, translated by Safi Kaskas and David Hungerford.

2 – *The Holy Qur'an*, translated by Abdullah Yusuf Ali.

3 – *The Qur'an: A New Translation*, translated by Tarif Khalidi.

4 – *The Majestic Quran: Guidance and Good news for the Mindful*, translated by Musharraf Hussein.

5 – *The Qur'an and Its Interpreters, Volume 2: The House of 'Imran*, by Mahmoud M. Ayoub, page 131-135.

6 – *Ihya' 'Ulum al-Din*, by Abu Hamid al-Ghazali, 4:339.

7 – *Qisas Al-Anbiya*, by Al-Iman Ibn Kathir (or possibly *Qisas Al-Anbiya*, by Ahmad Ibn Muhammad Thalabi or *Qisas Al-Anbiya*, by Muhammad Ibn Abd Allah Al-Kisai).

8 – *Diwan*, by Fakhr al-Din 'Iraqi.

9 – *I Called Through Your Door*, by Jelaluddin Rumi.

10 – *Anwar al-Tanzil wa-Asrar al-Ta'wil*, by Qadi Nasir al-Din al-Baydawi, Vol 2 (surahs 3-6), page 17.

11 – *Hadith*, Ṣaḥīḥ Muslim, 1015.

12 – *Hadith*, Ṣaḥīḥ al-Bukhārī, Vol. 4, Book 55, Hadith 641 and *Hadith*, Ṣaḥīḥ Muslim, 2366.

13 – *Hadith*, Ṣaḥīḥ al-Bukhārī, Vol. 4, Book 55, Hadith 657.

14 – *'Awarif al-Ma'arif*, by Shahib al-Din 'Umar al-Suhrawardi, 1:174.

References:

Ali, Abdullah Yusuf (2001, April). *The Holy Qur'an* (5th Edition). Hertfordshire, United Kingdom: Wordsworth Editions Limited.

Ali, Abdullah Yusuf (1938). *The Holy Qur'ān: English Translation & Commentary* (3rd Edition). Kashmiri Bazar, Lahore: Shaik Muhammad Ashraf.

Ayoub, Mahmoud (1992, May). *The Qur'an and Its Interpreters: Volume II: The House of 'Imran* (Paperback). Albany, NY: State University of New York Press.

Barks, Coleman (2011, December). *Rumi: The Big Red Book: The Great Masterpiece Celebrating Mystical Love and Friendship* (Paperback). San Francisco, CA: HarperOne.

Brinner, William M. (2002). *Lives of the Prophets ('Ara'is Al-Majalis Fi Qisas Al-Anbaya'): As Recounted By Abu Ishaq Ahmad Ibn Muhammad Ibn Ibrahim Al-Thalabi*. Leiden, The Netherlands: Brill.

Cragg, Kenneth (1999, February). *Jesus and the Muslim: An Exploration*. Oxford, United Kingdom: Oneworld Publications.

Gemeiah, Muhammad Mustapha (2006, July). *Stories of the Prophets: Written by Al-Imam ibn Kathir*. Riyadh, Saudi Arabia: Darussalam.

Haddad, Gibril Fouad (2016, July). *The Lights of Revelation & the Secrets of Interpretation: Hizb I of the Commentary on the Qur'an by al-Baydawi* (Paperback). Oldham, United Kingdom: Beacon Books.

Hussein, Musharraf (2021, April). *The Majestic Qur'an: Guidance and Good news for the Mindful*. Nottingham, United Kingdom: Invitation Publishing Ltd.

Karim, Fuzlul (2017). *Essential Ihya' 'Ulum al-Din: The Revival of the Religious Sciences, Volume I: Imam Al-Ghazali* (Revised). Kuala Lumpur, Malaysia: Islamic Book Trust.

Khalidi, Tarif (2003, April). *The Muslim Jesus: Sayings and Stories in Islamic Literature* (Paperback). Cambridge, MA: Harvard University Press.

Khalidi, Tarif (2009, September). *The Qur'an: A New Translation* (Paperback). New York, NY: Penguin Books.

Khan, Muhammad Muhsin (1997, June). *The Translation of the Meanings of Sahih Al-Bukhari: Arabic-English: Volume I-IX*. Riyadh, Saudi Arabia: Dar-us-Salam Publications.

Kaskas, Safi, & Hungerford, David (2016, January). *The Qur'an – with References to the Bible: A Contemporary Understanding*. Fairfax, VA: Bridges of Reconciliation.

Nurbakhsh, Javad (2012, July). *Jesus in the Eyes of The Sufis* (2nd Edition). USA: Khaniqahi Nimatullahi Publications.

Reference Qur'an Council (2021, March). *The Arabic-English Reference Qur'an: The First Translation of the Qur'an from the Original Arabic into Modern English with References to the Tawrah, Zabur, and Injil* (version 5.9).

Siddiqi, Abdul Hamid (1976, June). *Sahih Muslim: Volume I-IV*. Chicago, IL: KAZI Publications.

Smith, Paul (2018, May). *Divan of 'Iraqi*. New York, NY: CreateSpace Publishing.

Thackston Jr., Wheeler M. (1997, December). *Tales of the Prophets (Qisas Al-Anbiya'): Muhammad ibn 'Abd Allah Kisa'i*. Chicago, IL: KAZI Publications.

Wheeler, Brannon M. (2002, June). *Prophets in Islam: An Introduction to the Quran and Muslim Exegesis* (Paperback). New York, NY: Continuum.

❖ৰেৰেৰেৰেৰেৰে ❖

Qur'an Index

<table>
<tr><td>24</td><td>48</td></tr>
</table>

59 Al-Hashr

23	17

61 Al-Saff

6	48, 49
14	21, 48, 60

62 Al-Jumuah

1	17

66 Al-Tahrim

12	49

67 Al-Mulk

16	62
17	62

68 Al-Qalam

49	109, 126
50	109, 126

85 Al-Buruj

14	62

❖❀☙❀☙❀☙❀☙❀☙❀☙❖

Persons Index

Safi Kaskas/David Hungerford

Muhammad 47:24 – page 5

Yusuf Ali
Al-Fatihah 1:6 – page 12
Aal Imran 3:142 – page 40
Al-Aaraf 7:26 – page 101
Al-Hajj 22:37 – page 33, 126
Al-Mulk 67:16,17 – page 62
Al-Zukhruf 43:8 – pages 77-78

Tarif Khalidi
Al-Tawbah 9:5 – page 41
Ibrahim 14:34 – page 98
Al-Mulk 67:16,17 – page 62
Possible Tarif Khalidi
Al-Aaraf 7:188 – page 35

Musharraf Hussain
Luqman 31:27 – page 55

ISBN: 9798890086907